Ellie Russell lives in Lee-on-the-Solent on the south coast. She loves music, cookery, nature and is passionate about history. This is her first book.

FTDOFWSFY

DYFFM

Ellie Russell

ALL THE YOUNG DUDES

AUSTIN MACAULEY PUBLISHERS™

LONDON • CAMBRIDGE • NEW YORK • SHARJAH

A CIP catalogue record for this title is available from the British Library.

ISBN 9781528920018 (Paperback)
ISBN 9781528962162 (ePub e-book)

www.austinmacauley.com

First Published (2019)
Austin Macauley Publishers Ltd
25 Canada Square
Canary Wharf
London
E14 5LQ

Chapter 1
Starman

I will begin my story with the time when I first fell in love. My sexual awakening, as it were. The year was 1972 and I was twelve. I lived with my mother and stepfather, two sisters and brother, in a large three-storey house, in a small town on the south coast called Lee-on-the-Solent. My elder sister, Sarah, and I both went to the local grammar school. I was in the last year to sit the Eleven-plus. My brother, James, was seven and my other sister, Annie, was six.

Before we moved to Lee-on-the-Solent, we lived in a rented cottage in a small village called Isfield, in Sussex. James and Annie were born there. The cottage had no bathroom and no indoor toilet; we used a galvanised iron bath and a portable chemical loo. My stepfather had the unenviable task of regularly emptying this into a cesspit, which was located at the far end of the garden. Sarah and I loved sharing the bath in front of the fire. It can't have been much fun for the adults though. There was an outside toilet, but it was rarely used. It was a long way from the cottage and it stank. It had a large square wooden seat and was full of huge black cobwebs. Some of the spiders were as big as your head.

Sarah and I attended the local primary school. There were only two years, with about six pupils in each class. We could both read by the time we went to school and having such small classes gave us an excellent start. In those days, we used to be given little bottles of milk at morning break and I distinctly remember that in winter it would freeze solid in the bottles. In summer, the milk became unpleasantly warm, and the cream on top would congeal. Another vivid memory was marching in a line round and round the classroom whenever we sang *Onward Christian Soldiers* which, needless to say, was a firm favourite. I remember getting up at the crack of dawn to hunt for mushrooms on the village green, finding a dead snake (someone had decapitated it) in the lane behind our house and remember nearly killing my sister. That's a bit of an exaggeration, but she was badly hurt and it did entail a trip to the hospital. We were on the see-saw in the park, which was merely a long plank of wood balanced on a central support made of iron. There were little iron handles to hold on to. Although well weathered, the wood was untreated and we often came away with splinters which mother had to dig out with a needle. The whole play area was concrete. There was no soft rubber matting or thickly spread woodchip. Anyway, Sarah was up, and I was down when I suddenly thought it would be a splendid idea to jump off, which I did. She came crashing down, and the fall split her chin open. You have never seen so much blood; chins can sure bleed. She had to have several stitches and still has a scar. For days afterwards, you could clearly see the trail of blood leading from the park to our cottage.

My stepfather's mother and older brother lived just up the road from us. There was only one road running right through the village. They were simple country folk. There was always a dead rabbit or a brace of pheasant hanging from a hook outside the back door. My uncle was a man of very few words. He loved his allotment and grew masses of fruit and vegetables. He also kept chickens for eggs. I remember walking with him round the garden. He would point things out to me, patiently answering my never-ending questions and proudly showing me the plants in his greenhouse. He had a huge nose, like the beak of a parrot. He smoked a pipe and always wore dog-tooth check jackets with leather buttons and leather patches on the elbows. He was rather like Edward VIII, later Duke of Windsor to look at, only with a much bigger nose. Unlike Edward, he never found his Wallis. Apparently, he was engaged once—for 10 years! She obviously got tired of waiting or didn't like veg.

Every weekend, we used to make the long trek up the road for Sunday afternoon tea and a 'proper' bath. We ate in the cosy living room where there was a small black range fuelled by coal which provided what little heat there was in the house and in which Nan cooked their meals. There was a larger sitting room or parlour, but it was only used for wakes, important visitors like the doctor or at Christmas. It was very cold and full of overstuffed chairs with chintz covers. A large ornate clock ticked loudly on the mantle and chimed every hour on the hour, making us all jump. Upstairs were four large equally cold bedrooms. The beds all had huge feather pillows and each was covered with a plump eiderdown. Underneath every bed was a china chamber pot. Tea never varied. It was always salad with cold ham. In those days, salad consisted of lettuce (the floppy kind), cucumber and tomato. Invariably, you also got a slug and a good spattering of greenfly, sometimes a caterpillar. If you crunched on something, you had got a snail. There were none of the fancy salad leaves available now and no salad dressings. We used to sprinkle a little vinegar over the lettuce. There was no garlic to make a French dressing and olive oil was only available in tiny glass bottles from the Chemist. It was never used for cooking. Mother always had it handy for earaches. She would pour copious amounts into our ears and then plug them with a golf-ball size wad of cotton wool to prevent the oil from running out. To go with the ham, there was Pan Yan pickle (which you can still buy today). It was proper ham, lean and dry with an orange breadcrumb rind. The accompanying bread was homemade with a thick crust and was yeasty and delicious. Afterwards, there would be cake, also homemade, and tea poured from a large teapot into little china cups with saucers. I hated having a bath there. Nan was merciless with the soap and flannel. She would scrub us nearly raw paying particular attention to our ears which may go a long way to explain our frequent bouts of earache. She always had large bars of green Palmolive soap. The towels were thin and really rough, which removed a further layer of skin. The bathroom was absolutely freezing. All bathrooms were cold back then. There was no heating, unless you had a paraffin stove. Then you would be nice and warm but had to be a bit lively with your bath, lest you be overcome by the fumes. But all in all, they were halcyon days.

Sarah and I were born in Canada. Mother was a professional ice skater when she met and married my father. He was working for an insurance company. He was Jewish and was born in Czechoslovakia. At the beginning of WW2, the German army marched into Czechoslovakia and established a Slovakian Protectorate. My father and grandmother were interned at Sered, a forced labour camp about 60 km from Bratislava. He was seventeen. At some point, my father and a number of other male prisoners broke out and lived as partisans in the forest. It must have been truly awful for him having to leave his mother behind. Near the end of WW2, she was transported to Auschwitz and killed. It's poignant to see footage of old film, of Jews being herded into cattle trucks and peering through the barbed wire of concentration camp fences, clips we have all seen a thousand times and knowing that one of those women could be my actual grandmother. I don't know what happened to my grandfather, he may have survived the war. I do know that he was a doctor.

My parents' marriage was only ever going to fail. My mother was a spoilt rich kid brought up in a large house with a maid and a tennis court in a green and pleasant land and my father had seen hell up close and personal. When they separated, mother came back to England with my sister and me and moved to Sussex where my nan and gramps owned and ran The Laughing Fish Pub. Sarah and I adored the pub. We weren't allowed in either of the two bars, but I remember sneaking a peek and being fascinated by the stuffed fish in huge glass cases which were mounted on the walls. We would sit outside and gramps would bring us Coca-Cola in a bottle with a straw and some cheese and onion crisps. Sometimes, he would slip us a few maraschino cherries. The cola bottles were made of thick glass and were very ornate, and the crisps tasted so much better than they do today, although, they did go soggy more quickly. For a while, Nan and Gramps had a Lassie Collie dog called Scampy. He kept chasing sheep, and the local farmer threatened to shoot him on sight next time he did it, so they found him a new home. At least that's what we were told. I expect somewhere in Isfield, there's a farmer with a stuffed collie in a glass case mounted on his wall. A man called George helped out in the grounds. He always carried a dirty string mop and a metal bucket. You knew when he was coming, you could hear the clanking. He smelled strongly of Jeyes Fluid. It was here, helping out behind the bar, that my mother met my stepfather. The pub eventually became too much for my grandparents and they relocated to Lee-on-the-Solent on the south coast. When I was five, the house next door to them came up for sale, and we joined them there.

Like most fourteen-year-olds, Sarah was pop music mad and never went anywhere without a radio. Every morning, we had our breakfast to the accompaniment of Radio 1's *Tony Blackburn Show*. He featured a record of the week, which was always played at the same time each day and I would race downstairs to hear *Starman* by David Bowie. I loved that song; it stirred my very soul. I had no idea who David Bowie was or that he would shortly be stirring more than my soul, but I knew I loved that song. The sound of Tony Blackburn and the sight of my mother at the sink, furiously scraping charcoal from our toast was what I remember most fondly about the getting ready for school routine. I remember with less affection trying to warm a freezing cold cotton shirt over a single bar electric fire before putting it on over a vest and voluminous fleecy-lined pants. They were seriously big pants; Bridget Jones would have been proud. The shirt collar was so stiff that it was like a neck brace, the school tie making for added reinforcement. A bottle green sweater and a pleated skirt completed the ensemble. I also had long white socks and 'sensible' shoes. The other girls mostly wore straight skirts which hugged their hips and emphasised their figures, but mother insisted on pleated, and no amount of pleading would budge her. I used to roll the waistband over a few times to make the skirt shorter, but it just made the pleats fan out like a tutu. If mother was stressed, which she nearly always was, having our hair done was murder. She wielded the hard bristle brush and steel comb with more than a little malice aforethought, and don't get me started on the elastic bands. We had no nice soft scrunchies and hair ties back then. Our pony tails would be hauled so high and banded so tight, it gave you an instant face lift. Then metal hair grips would be rammed in to hold it all in place, carving a bloody furrow in your scalp. At the end of the day when you took the elastic band out, half your hair would come away and your head would feel tender and bruised for days. And there was always the burnt toast.

A must for my sister and me was *Top of the Pops* at 7.30pm on a Thursday. Sarah would turn up the TV and dance to every song, she was a great dancer. It was on *TOTP* that I first saw Bowie. Strumming his acoustic guitar, Mick Ronson playing the electric, their heads together as they harmonised and I fell absolutely and completely in love. He really was like someone from another planet with his thin face, bright red hair and those strange eyes. I thought he was the most beautiful man I had ever seen and I thought a lot of other thoughts as well. From that moment on, I was Bowie obsessed. I loved everything about him (except Angie of course. I loathed her with passion). I bought everything he had ever recorded and played it over and over. Our upstairs landing reverberated to the sound of *Space Oddity* and *The Man Who Sold the World*, clashing with *Curved Air and Cream* coming from my sister's room. I covered my bedroom with posters of him and generally mooned around. I remember getting *The Rise and Fall of Ziggy Stardust* and *The Spiders from Mars* for Christmas, and my friends clubbed together and bought *Hunky Dory* for my birthday. I had my straight blond hair, cropped and dyed. Of course, one couldn't buy the fabulous hair colours available now or the gels and putty. Maybe it was available in London and other big cities, but in Lee-on-the-Solent, it was Harmony Auburn or nothing. For wimps, there was 'Hint of a Tint'. I soon discovered henna which was a pain to apply but resulted in lovely bright orange hair. Imagine plastering your head in thick mud which smells of spinach and that's what applying henna was like. I managed to get it everywhere, up the walls, on the paintwork, over the floor, on all the towels—the whole bathroom was splattered with orange stains.

It was great having my grandparents living next door. They occupied the bottom half of the house adjoining ours and my aunt, uncle and cousins had the top half. My aunt was a real character. She trained as a ballet dancer but had mostly worked in the theatre either touring or in the West End. For a time, she worked at the famous Windmill Theatre in London. She could do the Can-Can, and that was more than enough to earn her my undying admiration. My uncle was her third husband, and father of two of my three cousins. He could kick a football into the air so high it was almost lost from sight. We kids never tired of watching him perform this feat, and whenever he was in his garden, we would produce a ball and pester him until he did it. Both my aunt and uncle liked to drink. A lot. Most nights they would amble round the corner to the pub, all smiles and bonhomie. Come closing time when they staggered out, things were not quite so cordial and the ensuing rows were loud enough to wake the dead and certainly the neighbours. Many times, mother would send my stepfather in to intervene before they did each other real damage. As soon as he left, they would start up again. I honestly think they enjoyed it.

Nanny had been a primary school teacher and was wonderful with children. She was intelligent and interesting and always fun to be around. She could read music and played the piano brilliantly. She could make dolls' clothes and fancy dress costumes. She could knit jumpers and slippers and make woolly pom-poms. She read us wonderful books and showed us how to make long paper chains of dancing men all joined together by their tiny paper hands. She taught us to crochet and do French knitting. She gave us slices of milk loaf, thickly spread with Lurpak butter and greengage jam. She would spend hours in her garden and knew the names of all the plants. She was especially fond of hostas and ferns. I loved her with all my heart. Living so close, she never got any rest. My cousin would turn up for her piano lesson, and as soon as she left, my sister and I would pop in and hot on our heels, my younger siblings. Nanny was always happy to see us. Or pretended to be. Grampy not so much! He used to say, "Can't you leave your nan alone for five minutes?" We couldn't. Nanny's name was Mabel, but Grampy called her Mamie. His name was Arnold.

My grandfather was wonderful too. We always called him Grampy. He had been a newspaper editor/journalist in London. In his early career, he was great friends with the cartoonist Giles who drew several cartoons of him now held in the British Cartoon Archive in Reading. Grampy had a big round face and wore round tortoiseshell spectacles. He looked quite a lot like Winston Churchill, but he smoked a pipe, not a cigar. I used to love watching him fill his pipe, tamping down the rich, moist tobacco which he kept in a pouch. He used to make little *pop, pop, pop* sounds with his mouth when lighting it up. I loved the smell of the smoke. I don't think my nan did. He used to sit in his favourite chair next to the fire, head resting against the white antimacassar. I don't know why Nanny put an antimacassar on his chair, he only had about six hairs, and I shouldn't think for a moment he put oil on them. Sarah and I used to stand at the back of his chair and count the hairs on his head out loud, giggling uncontrollably as we did so. We never tired of this game, but he took it all in good part. He had the most wonderful knack of encouraging us to eat the sort of food we would rather have had our fingernails pulled than put in our mouths. I think it was a mentality left over from rationing. He would rub his hands together and say, "Mmmmm, sheep eyes! Delicious. What a treat. Haven't had sheep eyes for years. What are we celebrating Mamie?" Only kidding; we didn't really eat sheep eyes, but Gramps would have probably enjoyed them. It was usually cabbage or some other food that children find repulsive. Sadly, Gramps died in his sixties. He had smoked nearly all his adult life and had chronic bronchitis. Nanny is also now long gone, but my uncle and aunt still live in the same house, although they own the whole building now.

To make some extra money, my mother did bed and breakfast. Nowadays, to do bed and breakfast, one has to have en-suites and everything has to be of the highest standard. Our guests just mucked in with the family, sharing the one bathroom (and there were six of us) and the two loos, neither of which were en-suite. If they wanted to watch TV, they sat in with us, and they ate with us too. I remember a Scottish man bringing us a haggis which mother cooked. It was horrible. I'm sure it had been in his duffle bag for weeks. He chatted away at dinner and none of us could understand a word he said; I'm not convinced he had a tongue. Mother nodded and made polite 'mmm' noises, but it was very difficult. Sometimes, mother would rent our rooms, and we had to camp on the landing. We did have regulars though who came each year, so they must have enjoyed the experience. Either that or we were very cheap. Each year, we took in French students. I adored one of them. He looked like Woody Allen and was extremely fussy about his clothes, his food and etiquette in general. He only drank milk, and that had to be at room temperature. His socks had to be made from real wool. He wore funny little leather slippers and played himself at chess. I christened him 'Nice' because that's what I thought he was and I always called him that. I never left the poor man alone, and it didn't occur to me that he might have found me a bit of a nuisance. I sewed up the bottom of his pyjamas so he couldn't get his legs in. I squirted him with a water filled Jiffy lemon secreted up my sleeve when he was watching TV, and I snuck into his room and rearranged his chess men. He was always tutting and saying "Merde" under his breath and often not under his breath but the torment continued. He did come back year after year, until we moved, in fact, so he couldn't have minded me too much.

I loved the autumn. Halloween was wonderful. Mother would help us carve pumpkins into lanterns with ghoulish faces. We would place a tea light inside to be lit when it got dark. We would wash and dry the hundreds of discarded pumpkin seeds ready to be dyed and strung into necklaces, which no one ever wore. I painted everything and anything with luminous paint. The result was always a massive disappointment. Frankly, a glow worm would have emitted more light. Nanny made us witch's hats out of black paper and card on to which we stuck silver moons and stars. Under the brim, she hung long strands of grey wool to replicate witch's hair. Black costumes were hastily cobbled together, and Sarah and I would dance about, trying to scare the younger children. Every year mother made toffee apples, and every year they were inedible. Nanny's chocolate fudge was much more successful. We didn't go trick or treating. It wasn't as popular then, and I think mother thought it tantamount to begging.

Hot on the heels of Halloween came bonfire night. My stepfather usually began building the bonfire early in October. It was huge. We would make a guy, stuffing a pair of his old trousers and a jumper with large wads of newspaper. We formed a head by stuffing the gusset of a pair of tights and added a cardboard mask for the face. Then the guy would be fixed to an old wooden chair and with a fair amount of difficulty hoisted to the top of the fire. Every year, the bonfire had to be doused with at least gallon of petrol to get it going as it was always damp, but that was part of the ritual. It made a very satisfying 'whoosh' as it ignited and the flames leapt up the pyre. I always think it a shame that Guy Fawkes' effigy is burnt. I think it should be hung, drawn and quartered. You could get some entrails from the butcher and stuff them up his jumper (the guy not the butcher). It would certainly be more historically accurate and I think your average kid would find it a whole lot more thrilling. We watched the fireworks with all the usual 'oohing and aahing'. We made swirling patterns and wrote our names in the black night air with our sparklers. The Catherine Wheels were always a non-event. My stepfather used to fix them to the shed door with big nails, but they only ever managed half a rotation at best. Then it was sausages and jacket potatoes before bed.

Once bonfire night was over, the agonisingly long wait for Christmas began, but there were plenty of preparations to keep us busy. Mother had already filled a shelf in the larder with Kilner jars packed full of pickled onions, red cabbage and green tomato chutney. The mouth-watering aroma of vinegar and pickling spices permeated the air, wafting right to the very top of the house. The rich Christmas fruit cake had been made. I remember watching mother weighing out the ingredients, the dark Muscovado sugar, the dried fruit and the candied peel. She always added a generous slug of brandy. We all had a stir of the mixture and then a fight over who would lick the bowl. Once the cake had been allowed a few weeks to mature, mother covered it with marzipan. Then we all helped with the decoration. Mother always made the icing rough, to look like snow she said. I can't remember when I last saw snow that was rough. I don't think she could do smooth. The icing on our birthday cakes was always rough. We all wanted to add our own artistic flourish so the finished cake did look rather busy, crowded with miniature robins, snowmen and Santas in various poses, but we were pleased with our efforts.

All of us children made paper chains. We would sit on the hall floor in the middle of an ever growing pile of rustling coloured rings, happily licking and sticking to our hearts content. The little ones could be rather overzealous with the licking which prevented the sticking, but eventually, we had enough. The colours weren't very true; I think the manufacturers might have used vegetable dye, but they looked nice when they were up. My stepfather would climb his high stepladder and we would hand him the completed chains. He would wobble about, balancing precariously whilst trying to attach them to the ceiling with drawing pins which he held in his mouth. We always had a real tree, which my sister and I chose. It was also our job to collect the turkey, and because we were a large family, it was a big one. We used to trundle my go-cart down the road to pick it up as it was far too heavy to carry. We always got a six-foot tree, and it stood in the bay window of our front room. Back then, you couldn't get a tree stand, so a bucket filled with earth was pressed into service. We covered the bucket with red crepe paper. Inevitably, the tree ended up listing, and the lights had usually stopped working on the first day, but we thought it looked lovely. Sarah and I would decorate it, happily unwrapping the delicate baubles which had been packed away the year before, each little glass orb greeted with delight like an old familiar friend. Some had seen better days and were worn and dull, but we always found a place for them on the tree. We would load on so many baubles and so much tinsel, you couldn't see the tree anymore—there could have been anything underneath. We completed our masterpiece by lobbing on small pieces of cotton wool to represent snow, and of course, we put the fairy on top. I seem to remember she was missing an arm.

It took me ages to go sleep on Christmas Eve, as by then, my excitement had reached fever pitch. I knew it was my stepfather who delivered the stockings. I recognised his slow weary tread on the stairs. Santa would have fair bounded up. Lying in my warm bed, feeling the promising weight and wiggling my toes to make that stocking crinkle was the best feeling in the world. By 5am, I was up and into Sarah's room where I would hop into her bed and we opened our stockings together. We always got rather a lot of Avon toiletries. There was invariably a 'Pretty Peach' soap-on-a-rope and matching talc. Around this time of year, mother became an Avon Lady to earn a little extra. Both Sarah and I thought it a little too coincidental that Santa carried so much Avon in his sack, but maybe he was working for them too. Much to my disgust, we were made to have a decent breakfast before opening our presents. Present opening was pretty chaotic. We were supposed to each take a turn to open something, but it usually ended up in a free-for-all with paper flying everywhere. My stepfather always tried to look pleased with his new socks and pants. I had always, always found, examined and often played with most of my presents, a good few weeks before Christmas Day. I think mother thought they were well hidden, but I knew exactly where they were, right at the very back of the cupboard under the stairs in her bedroom. It didn't spoil things for me at all knowing what I had got, I preferred it. I'm not big on surprises. She was very good; we usually got exactly what we had asked for. When presents were over, we would join Nan and Gramps, and the adults would have a sherry. If my aunt and uncle joined us, they would have several. Then it was back to our house for dinner. I'm always puzzled by the fact that a large turkey today cooks in a few hours. Back then, everybody either cooked their bird on a low heat overnight or got up at dawn to get it started. Mother got up at dawn. Maybe the ovens weren't as hot in those days, or maybe mother was anticipating one of the many electricity cuts prevalent in the '70s. In any event, the turkey was annihilated but the sprouts were too, so it balanced out nicely. After dinner, my stepfather would try and fail to set the Christmas pudding alight. The pudding contained real sixpences—none of this health and safety rubbish, you just spat your teeth out and carried on eating.

I was a real tomboy. I loved being outdoors and was always up a tree, riding my bike or roller skating. My skates had a rubber brake at the back, and all the pavements around the block were covered in long black rubber skid marks. Stilts made by my stepfather were also a great favourite, as was my space hopper. There were hardly any cars around, so we played quite happily on the road. We loved dressing up and had a large trunk full of clothes. During the summer, we swam most days either in the sea or the open air pool. I remember thinking I could do a sneaky poo in the sea. I thought I had got away with it until it bobbed up and floated behind me like a torpedo locked on to its target. Thinking back, it always seems that the summers were long and hot and everything was good. It probably wasn't like that; it must have rained sometimes. I know I spent every summer covered from head to foot in calamine lotion which was like liquid chalk, as I was fair and burnt. Needless to say, most of my friends went a lovely nut brown.

Our cat, Lucky, was a horror. His mother was feral, and Lucky had been born under a neighbour's hedge. His litter mates were despatched by the neighbour—drowned I think, hence the rather unoriginal name. He was never tamed. Mind you, the said neighbour neutered him without anaesthetic, so maybe that was why he was so tetchy. He could really scratch and bite. I'm talking deep gouges, plenty of blood and pain. He would lie hidden in bushes and ambush you when you walked by, shooting out and removing good chunk of flesh from your legs. Then, in a flash, he was gone, leaving you badly shaken and bleeding profusely. As he got older and slightly more trusting, he would sit on your lap, and if this happened, you would keep very, very still, sometimes for hours. If you moved, he would have you.

Often if you didn't move, he would have you. If you tried to touch him anywhere but the top of his head, he would have you. Once mother took him to the vet and they had to throw a basket over him. He bit the vet (badly) and the vet told mother not to bring him again. Every day without fail during the spring and summer, the cry would go up at some point, "Lucky's got a bird/frog/mouse/rat/rabbit." He killed almost every pet hamster we ever had and we had a lot (all called Hammy). He killed our budgie (mother told us Ted had flown away and was living happily in the trees), and he blinded my gerbil in one eye. If mother dropped her guard for a second in the kitchen, he would make off with chops or other cuts of meat which she was preparing for dinner. Sometimes mother gave chase and managed to retrieve the meat, in which case, it would be rinsed, cooked and served up to my stepfather. He never seemed to notice that his pork chop looked a little ragged. We didn't have a cat flap. I'm not sure if they had been invented then. Our back door had a window and if Lucky wanted to come in, he would spring up and hang by his claws on the small ledge underneath. When you opened the door, he would still be hanging, stuck fast by his claws until he could manage to retract them. Then he would drop down and walk in with great dignity as if to say, "Well that wasn't at all embarrassing." Often when we went out, he would follow us, trotting happily behind, sometimes for quite a distance until one of us would have to turn back and lead him home. All my friends were terrified of Lucky as were all the neighbouring cats and probably a high percentage of the dogs as well. One friend refused to come to our house anymore because Lucky had ambushed her so often. He was certainly unique and I thought he was great. I also had two rabbits called Pip and Patch, two mice called Mungo and Jerry, a one-eyed gerbil called Mattie Brown and a new goldfish virtually every week. Lucky kept eating them.

Although my head swum with dreams of David Bowie, I did have a real boyfriend. I honestly can't remember where I met him, he didn't go to my school. He was tall and thin with floppy light brown hair, and I thought I was in love. Not as in love as with DB, you understand, but Paul was very much second best. We often lay together on my little single bed, occasionally kissing, nothing passionate, no tongues. Sarah and I had separate bedrooms on the top floor of our big old house. It was easy to sneak people up the two flights stairs without Mother knowing—she was always busy in the kitchen. So my sister entertained a steady flow of bikers and I entertained Paul. I also practised smoking Consulate menthol cigarettes and applying makeup for the first time. Hot pants were all the rage as were maxi dresses. Sarah had lovely long legs and owned two amazing pairs of hot pants made of PVC; one pair were bright yellow, and one pair the colour of milky coffee. Mother bought me a pair of what can only be described as lederhosen, in purple velvet. The shorts came nearly to my knees and the bib to my chin. Luckily, I had a pair of very short shorts that I had worn in junior school which I thought looked rather sexy over black tights. I used to put my coat on overtop and sneak out; mother would have had a fit if she had seen what I was wearing. I had also taken to wearing a bra. I'm not sure why. I had nothing to put in it. I think it was a size 30AAAA or something like that. I stuffed it with cotton wool which gave me a pair of very small bumps. Around this time, mother supplied me with my first sanitary wear. This comprised an elastic belt which fastened round the waist from which hung two suspenders one front, one back. On to these, you hooked your sanitary pad, which swung hammock-like between your legs. It was large and padded and could have stood in for a pillow if you were short of one. It was so bulky that it was impossible to put your legs together, so you would walk like a cowboy. It was devoid of even a scrap of lace to make it more feminine being the horrible yellowy colour of undyed cotton. It went straight into the bin until I could get hold of some Tampax.

But back to my boyfriend. We had been invited to a friend's party. Almost every weekend, someone's poor unsuspecting parents went away, and their teenage offspring would have a party. There was always something going on. Parents would come home to carpets awash with beer, fag butts, roaches and more often than not the odd pool of vomit. But this was not that sort of party. We were only twelve (there weren't any roaches), and as I remember, we ended up playing postman's knock. Teams would be split into boys and girls, and someone would go out of the room. A bottle was spun, and whoever it pointed at would have to join the person outside and kiss them. Usually this would involve a whole lot of giggling and a quick peck (sometimes followed by a retching impression). On this occasion, my friend was outside and the bottle landed on Paul. Out he went, and we waited and waited and waited and waited until eventually they both appeared looking rather dishevelled and somewhat sheepish. After that, for the rest of the time, they were conspicuous by their absence. On the way home, Paul dumped me. He said Kathy was a much better kisser.

Sarah had more luck and a steady stream of admirers which caused a good deal of friction between her and my stepfather. She and her friends (often numbering double figures) would sit around our large kitchen table chatting late into the night. All the lights would be blazing, the kettle constantly boiling and vast amounts of tea and coffee made and drank. This really niggled my stepfather. He was always moaning about the expense and threatening to turn the electric off and hide the coffee, but no one took any notice. The other bone of contention was the telephone. Kids don't know how lucky they are now to have mobile phones. They can have private conversations. We had to stand in the hall where the whole house could hear you talking to your friends. No doubt, your friends hear your father shouting, "Get off that bloody phone. Do you think I'm made of money?" Everyone knew when your boyfriend phoned, and worse, everyone knew when he didn't and would witness your heartbreak. And it was heartbreak that was heading our way. My mother called us together and announced that she and my stepfather were divorcing. My sister and I had been aware for a while that all was not rosy between them. We heard them at night yelling at each other. We used to creep down and sit at the top of the stairs where we could listen to them rowing in the kitchen. We would huddle together in our dressing gowns, white-faced and wide-eyed. We could hear everything. It wasn't pleasant. At one time, I think they might have actually come to blows. There was definitely the sound of a slap. I think my mother was seeing someone else. So, my parents were splitting up, I had been told I was a crap kisser, and we were going to have to move.

I was devastated to be leaving our beautiful old house. I wasn't in the least upset at losing my stepfather as we weren't close. Of course, it was hard on James and Annie as he was their dad, and they adored him. Don't get me wrong, he wasn't nasty to us or anything, but he never treated Sarah and me as his own.

From the moment when he had first married my mother, Sarah hated him with every fibre of her being. She was desperately unhappy about not knowing our real father. To this day, she has never forgiven my mother for failing to arrange access to him. If I am honest, I was quite happy not to have my father around. All my friends had to ask their fathers if they could go here or there, or do this or that. I just did what I wanted, and I thought it was great. Mother was very naïve and believed anything we told her. Perhaps it was a case of anything for a quiet life, or maybe I am just a very good liar (actually I think it's the latter). I was also quite relieved not to have gone through school with my real surname which was Seeman as I would have been called 'Spunky' for sure. Now I am old, and with each passing year, I long to have known my father. He died in 1988, so we will never meet, but one day I hope to visit his grave in Israel. I have some photos of him which I cherish.

It wasn't long before the house was sold. On the last night, I walked slowly around the now empty rooms and whispered goodbye to my home. I said goodbye to the walls, the light switches, the mantelpieces, the cavernous larder, the old Victorian toilets with their long chains dangling from high rise cisterns, the huge hallway and those wonderful two flights of stairs. I touched everything as I said my farewell. I said goodbye to my little room with its sloping attic ceiling now patchy where sellotape had once held up my Bowie posters. My little bedroom where I had played for hours with my trolls, catalogued my large collection of tropical shells, listened to my records and practised blowing smoke down my nose. I bade it farewell. I looked out of the top landing window and tried to burn the image into my memory. I crept into the loft which was accessed via a door next to my bedroom and smelt for the last time, the mustiness of dust and old wooden beams. I had spent so much time in that attic, making dens and rummaging around. It was full of treasures. A lamp in the shape of an old galleon, large stiff sails, brittle and yellow with age. An ancient set of encyclopaedias with blue leather covers. Numerous old suitcases covered in tatty stickers of destinations visited long ago and mother's white leather ice skates with their green wooden blade-guards. I always burnt a candle for light, sometimes several—how I didn't start a fire with all the dry wood about, I'll never know. The large airing cupboard on our top landing also made a good den. It housed a huge galvanised iron water tank, often with drowned and bloated spiders floating on top, occasionally a mouse.

I remembered the day when we first moved in. We had travelled up from Sussex in a huge removal van packed with our belongings, Lucky protesting loudly from inside a cardboard box. I remembered swinging on the front gate, watching the men carrying in our furniture. The house was huge, so much to explore. We thundered up the two flights of stairs, bagged our bedrooms, opened all the doors; it was so exciting. When we had first arrived, the front garden was full of straggly rose bushes which although badly in need of pruning, filled the air with their heady perfume. Fragrant sweet alyssum and peppery aubrietia had seeded itself in the cracks of the red and yellow tiled front path. There was a lawn and flower bed to the side of the house and a vast garden at the back full of fruit trees, raspberry canes, gooseberries and large clumps of golden rod jostling with crocosmia and shasta daisies. There was an enormous fuchsia bush. Before they opened, the flower buds could be squeezed to make a very satisfying pop, like nature's bubble wrap— wonderful. I used to make daisy chains on the grass and hunt amongst the large patches of clover for one with four leaves. There was an air-raid shelter with a flat reinforced concrete roof and a garden shed which housed all our bikes and the bales of straw for my rabbits. My stepfather cut a small cat size square out of the shed door at the bottom, so Lucky had somewhere to shelter if the weather turned bad and no one was around to let him in. Saying goodbye was terribly painful. In my mind's eye, I can still walk through every bit of that house, and I often do at night before I drop off to sleep. I can remember every room, every floor covering, every stick of furniture and every hidey-hole. I still remember our telephone number which is strange because I can't remember any of the other phone numbers I've had over the years. It's probably because I was polite back then and recited the number each time I answered the phone. Nowadays I just say, "What?" I often see our old house as I still live in Lee. My aunt and uncle still live next door. It has changed a lot (not for the better if you ask me). If I ever win the lottery, I'll make the owners an offer they can't refuse, that's for sure. I'd give anything to spend another night in my little attic bedroom up those two flights of stairs. I might even put up a Bowie poster and smoke a Consulate.

Chapter 2
Baby Driver

So, belongings packed and with Lucky protesting loudly in his cardboard box, we moved to Gosport. The people who bought our house said they would take on my rabbits, as there wasn't room for them where we were going. I bet they went straight into a pie.

The new house was an end terrace on a busy main road. It took me a long time to get used to the sound of the traffic thundering past my window day and night; the buses were especially frequent and noisy. I hated it. Sarah refused to move there and promptly found a place to share with her boyfriend. She was only sixteen. I still had my own bedroom which was right at the front of the house in what should have been the first reception room. There was a tiled fireplace, which I promptly sprayed silver, and I stuck black felt stars to the ceiling with superglue. The next owners probably had to replaster the ceiling to get rid of them. I didn't ask permission, just did it. I painted all my furniture black, and I had a black leather-effect sofa under the window. I had two funky lights, bought at the Ideal Home Exhibition in London, one with a red bulb and one with a blue bulb. I had also acquired a state of the art record deck and speakers so my music sounded fabulous. My beloved posters and plenty of black ostrich feathers completed the room, and it looked lovely—well I thought so, I expect it gave mother a bit of a turn. Outside was a short passage and then another small room which became the family living room. Another little room, kitchen and tiny bathroom with loo completed the ground floor.

Mother quickly married her new beau, who was absolutely horrible. I can't even begin to imagine what she saw in him. He was fat and sat around in a string vest. He wore horrible nylon shirts and cheap suits and was always making himself fry ups. I think he only liked fried food. He had one bath a week and really smelly feet. I wouldn't even put my clothes in the laundry bin in case a pair of his socks were lurking in there. None of us liked him. Well mother did at first, but that didn't last. My younger sister, Annie, really hated him. I went right off the rails at this time and started to skip school in a big way. In fact, I was rarely there. I went from a bright, top of the class, grammar school girl to the worst truant in the area (so I was told). My mood was dark. I was in a dark place. When I skipped school, I sat in the public toilets and smoked; it wasn't as if I was doing anything interesting. I felt bored and unfulfilled. The grammar had been merged with the local secondary school to form a large comprehensive and I was lost in the crowd. The truant officer was rubbish, but he did seem to patrol his beat diligently, as whenever I stepped onto the open road to make a break for it, he suddenly appeared in his little blue car. He was certainly dedicated. He must have lain in wait for hours. There was no attempt at understanding or counselling back then; you just got a stern bollocking. You were made to feel like Public Enemy Number One. It only made me even more determined not to bow to pressure and the skipping of school continued.

I had a huge crush on a man I had seen around. I would often spot him driving his silver-blue Ford Capri. His name was Tom, and I was smitten. He cruised around, his friend in the passenger seat, Bowie's music blaring through the open window, eyeing up girls. To this day, I can still remember the registration number of his car. He had his hair cut like Bowie and dyed bright purple. His sister was in my year at school, but I didn't know her, only who she was. I was on constant high alert and watched out for him like a hawk. I know I did an awful lot of walking up and down the road. I was always volunteering to go to the local shop. One day, he stopped and offered me a lift, and I was over the moon. I found out where he lived, and I think I just rolled up and rang the bell. He asked me in, and we went into his bedroom. He told me to get undressed, and we got into bed. I remember seeing his penis and being really surprised. I thought he must have shaved it, as all the girls at school said men had hairy willies. I reasoned that it was probably something a Bowie fan would do. I was also amazed at how rigid it was. There was no attempt at foreplay. He did the deed (took all of a minute), and I lay there frozen, not knowing what was going on. He didn't use a condom or ask if I was on the pill. He didn't chat with me or ask to see me again. I don't think he even kissed me. I was just fourteen, and he in his mid-twenties. Afterwards, we got dressed, and he showed me out, or more precisely shoved me out. I was happy to have lost my virginity, and I hugged the knowledge to myself as he drove me home. I was rather sore and tender down below and a bit squelchy—but I was officially a woman.

Nanny died. I felt guilty because since we had moved and I had discovered the opposite sex, I had hardly been to see her. I suppose that's kids for you. One minute, they need you for everything, the next, they've found something more interesting. I think of her often; she practically brought my sister and me up; she was a wonderful lady. Hers was the first funeral I had been to. I was too young when Grampy died. It was pretty awful. I remember how small the coffin looked and the horrendous non-descript piped music. I wanted to scream at the person who gave the eulogy, "You didn't even know her. Stop talking about her as if you did." Then that dreadful moment when the curtains closed and the coffin is forever lost from view. I was glad when it was over. Generally, I was terribly unhappy at this time. I tried several attempts at suicide. One time, I swallowed a whole bottle of disprins. I was dreadfully sick. The tablets tasted a whole lot worse coming up than going down. A mass of regurgitated bitterness—and carrots of course. I spewed all over my bedroom rug which I rolled up and threw away. I felt really, really ill for about three days. I had ringing in my ears, and my vision was blurred, but I never told anyone.

I had very low self-esteem. I never felt as worthy as other people. I felt different but not in a good or positive way. Until the age of eleven, I had asthma which I had developed at around 18 months old. There were no inhalers then, and I was hospitalised on numerous occasions. I clearly remember being in a high-sided hospital cot and screaming for mother as she left me. It must have been truly difficult for her too. The nurses were all super-efficient and rather brusque. They made no attempt whatsoever to comfort the children in their care. I was given a drug called Ethedrine which is widely used in the manufacture of crystal meth. This may go a long way to explain my later love of pharmaceuticals and problems with addiction—I started early.

Because I was so poorly for so much of the time, my sister had to grow up quickly. It wasn't anyone's fault but was hard on her nevertheless.

I was prescribed Tetracycline, a drug which causes staining to developing teeth. My adult teeth came through grey with a dark band through the middle. This made me incredibly self-conscious and unhappy. Some of the boys at school called me 'green teeth'. I always smiled with my mouth tight shut, a bit like Frank Spencer in *Some Mother's Do 'Av 'Em.* Of course I knew the staining was deep inside my teeth, but it didn't prevent me from scrubbing them relentlessly to try to make them white. Someone told me that in olden days they used to use soot to clean their teeth as it was so abrasive, and I tried it. I also tried using bleach. My teeth remained grey, and my gums receded. I told mother over and over how I felt. She should have acknowledged that my teeth were bad and maybe said we could do something about it when I was older, but all she ever said was: "Your teeth are lovely. There's nothing wrong with them." This was her stock answer to everything—catastrophic haircuts, frizzy perms, massive face boils, dreadful clothes. "You look lovely," she would say. I would have expected her to have empathy. As a young woman, she was very beautiful. She did some modelling and adorned the covers of a couple of well-known magazines. She was always immaculately turned out. I remember watching her putting on her makeup and being totally fascinated. She always wore bright red lipstick, applied carefully with a lip brush and then powdered and blotted. She pulled some very odd faces. She also had beautiful straight white teeth. Mother never seemed to get that kids just want to be like all the other kids. In primary school, not only did I have to contend with green teeth and a chronic wheeze, she made me wear a bodice over my vest for warmth. I think she brought a supply over from Canada. It was like the Kevlar stab-vests worn by the police. And my vest worn underneath, it was cream with SLEEVES! All the other children had lovely snowy white (sleeveless) vests; it made me feel awful. I felt dirty inside.

Maybe because we didn't have a car, we never went to the popular shops in town to get clothes but shopped locally. That meant the 'Ladybird Shop' where most things were made of polyester, and everything was in a colour that no sane person would think of putting a child in. Mother liked the fact that we were served. I'm convinced the shop owner took perverse delight in seeing our stricken faces when she whipped each item off the shelves or out of drawers with a flourish to show my mother. All our clothes had to have 'room for growing'. I'm not talking a bit of slack, oh no, it had to be at least three years' worth. She bought my bathing suit there. My friend had the most gorgeous bikini. It was white with fringing. It was tiny and fitted perfectly; she had a slim tanned little body, and she looked really nice. My bikini (and I use the word loosely) consisted of a pair of shorts which came up to my belly button, in navy blue with a jaunty belt and large bow in a lime green and white stripe. The top was all lime green/white stripe and was ruched so it just looked as though you should have had a bosom to fill it, which of course being a kid you didn't. It was probably made of polyester. I hated that shop. I hated that bikini. Mother's next favourite shop was the Co-op, which was stocked with equally old-fashioned, frumpy clothes. She liked the fact that she could clad us in something truly horrible and get dividend stamps. It was a huge store, reminiscent of Grace Bros. In *Are You Being Served* and like Grace Bros. we were usually the only customers. It closed down soon after. Probably about the time we started buying our own clothes. When I first started senior school, for while I had to wear my cousin's grey gaberdine mac. Bear in mind that the school colour was bottle green and also that my cousin was 9 years older than me, which will give you some idea of how big that mac was. I looked like Inspector Clouseau. It bordered on child abuse. To add insult to injury, my stepfather made me a basket to use when I had domestic science, to carry the food I made home in. I say basket, it was a large oblong wooden box with a large wooden handle. It would have made a great coffin for a dead dog. It had a very homemade look to it and an overpowering smell of varnish. It caught everyone's shins and weighed a ton, especially when full of my none too light cakes. Of course, all the other girls in the class had light, neat little wicker baskets.

Music was everything to me. I played it constantly. Mostly Bowie, but I also adored Queen, Pink Floyd, Supertramp, Cockney Rebel, Lou Reed, Iggy Pop and Alice Cooper. I loved shoes and was proud owner of some silver leather boots with really high platforms. I wore the boots to school with a floor length tiger print coat and was immediately sent home (that worked well)! My friend owned a pale grey silk Victorian corseted jacket, and I borrowed this a lot. I had each ear double pierced which didn't please mother, who thought only gypsies and pirates pierced their ears. Also, to her horror, to look more like my idol, I shaved off my eyebrows. I dyed my hair black for a while but soon went back to red. I had my front teeth veneered, so at last I could smile. That year, I saw Bowie in a concert for the first time at Southampton Gaumont. He didn't disappoint. I screamed myself hoarse. I also saw Steve Harley & Cockney Rebel and Queen in Southampton. Freddie had long hair back then!

Chapter 3
Burning Love

At last, school was getting better, and things were looking up. I had seen a boy who had made my stomach flip. In fact, every time I saw him, my tummy did several somersaults and my heart would beat wildly in my chest. He was in the year above me. His name was Aaron. He had high cheekbones, brown eyes and long, dark hair which was quite curly. They were great curls, not tight or frizzy but long and loose just resting on his shoulders. He had a great smile. I thought he was gorgeous. He went around in a group with three other boys. They all wore the same padded jackets, and they were always together. You could hear them long before you could see them. Whenever they saw me, they would call out, "Hey, Ziggy," which I thought was kinda nice. Aaron always flirted with me in that teasing half compliment, half insult way schoolboys have. His great and enduring love was Elvis 'the King' Presley, and he would sing Elvis at every available opportunity, usually substituting his own words like, "Oh I just can't help believing, when she slips her hand down my trousers…" Pure class. After a while, we got together. I can't remember the details which is odd because I was so happy. We were together for about two weeks when he threw me over for a girl called Sue with massive knockers. By that time, I had developed myself and was no slouch in the boob department (they've headed south a bit now), but hers were seriously big; two great melons, a teenage boy's dream, and I couldn't compete. I remember crying and crying. I was inconsolable. At least, he hadn't told me I couldn't kiss. It was just that my tits weren't up to scratch.

Life went on. I had a couple of boyfriends. A hippy who smelt of Patchouli oil and wore an Afghan coat which smelt strongly of goat. When it got wet, it smelt like a herd of goats.

He was a lot like Neil in the Young Ones. He even said 'far out' a lot. I tired of him quickly—I never did like joss sticks. There was a chap called Edward who had really long hair and was handsome and very sweet—too sweet for me and too quiet, he had to go. Also, he lived with his gran, and the house smelt of mothballs which was a bit of a turn-off. I liked one chap called Ray. He was plumpish, ginger and freckled but kind of cute. He had dimples, and dimples improve any face (it's when you've got them on your thighs you have to worry). One evening, he took me to a houseboat which he had borrowed from a friend. At least I think he borrowed it, he might have just broken in. We played *Young Americans* on a loop and made out pretty much all night. Whenever I hear *Young Americans*, I think of our night of passion on the houseboat and inwardly chuckle. It is still one of my favourite songs. So, nice one Ray—a gold star performance, you are fondly remembered.

Mother never knew where I was or who I was with. She was incredibly lax. I had no supervision at all. At one point, she did try to put her foot down about my smoking, but it didn't stop me, not for a moment. It was the easiest thing in the world to tell her I was staying the night with a girlfriend, and no questions were ever asked. Maybe it was because she had led such a sheltered life and had no clue what the average teenager was capable of when left to their own devices, I don't know. I thought it was brilliant at the time. I was smoking and drinking and staying with boyfriends. I thought I was having fun, but really I was damaging myself in oh so many ways.

I had a friend called Stuart who I adored. I knew he was hopelessly in love with me, but I could never have been physical with him. I just didn't find him attractive in that way. He was incredibly funny; he made me laugh and laugh, and we got on so well. The comedy double act Peter Cook & Dudley Moore used to play a couple of hapless characters called Derek & Clive. They had made an eponymous album of sketches. It was hysterically funny but very, very rude, even by today's standards. You certainly couldn't play it when your parents were within earshot. Stuart's voice sounded exactly like Peter Cook's Clive. Just hearing him speak reduced me to helpless giggles. He lived near to me and rented a room in a house with a hippy couple. The house was full of beaded curtains, bean bags and incense burners.

All the rooms were painted in outlandish colours. Naturally, they were vegetarians. His landlady used to make a wholemeal pastry flan topped with a spicy bean mixture. Surprisingly, it was rather tasty, and Stuart always shared it with me. He did seem to get it for dinner an awful lot. Maybe it was all she could cook. Stuart was crazy about the Beatles and in particular, John Lennon. I used to make him play *Here, There and Everywhere* from their album *Revolver* over and over again. Had I only but realised it, I would have probably been much happier with someone like Stuart. However, I was shallow back then and physical attraction rated highly for me. Nowadays, I would be more likely to plump for a man who could make me laugh and just pop a bag over their head. I regret hurting Stuart. Although I truly enjoyed his company, I led him on and used him to bolster my flagging self-confidence. I hope he's happy now. I like to think that some nice girl somewhere is making him spicy bean flans and laughing at his jokes.

My best friend was called Sylvia. We were inseparable from the age of about eight to eighteen, when our lives took different paths. She was incredibly pretty. She looked very much like Agnetha in Abba, only not quite so blond. Her hair was golden brown with natural highlights. It was poker straight and hung down to the small of her back. She had a neat little upturned nose and a wide, sexy mouth. All the coolest boys fancied Sylvia. She was spoilt for choice. She never went out with the same lad for more than a couple of weeks, and I don't think I can remember one single instance when he was the one who finished it, such was the kudos of being her boyfriend. I, on the other hand, was dumped with such startling regularity, one might have expected I would get used to it, maybe even come to like it. I didn't have much luck with the opposite sex. I always had a boyfriend but never the ones I really wanted. Of course having a stunningly beautiful best mate didn't help. Somehow I always felt like the booby prize. Sometimes, life sucks! The trouble with Sylvia was that she could frequently be moody, and then she wasn't nice to be around. You could cut the atmosphere as they say. She was so rude to her mother it made your hair stand on end. It was because of her rudeness that my mother didn't like Sylvia at all. Sylvia however seemed to like our family very much indeed. During the weekends and school holidays, she virtually lived at our house.

Every morning, she would cycle round to call for me. I was never up; it's only in later years that I've managed to emerge from my bed before noon without causing myself trauma. So Sylvia would perch on the end of my bed, chatting away until I finally got up. Then she would accompany me to the bathroom whilst I washed and brushed my teeth.

When we moved to Gosport, she would come for a sleepover practically every weekend. Her father would drop her off, and she would arrive carrying her little portable black and white TV. On Saturday night, we would make ourselves a Vesta packet meal, which we thought was the height of culinary excellence and sophistication. Vesta had several different options. Beef curry, chicken curry, chow mein, chop suey, risotto and paella. The box had a picture of the finished meal on the front which bore no resemblance whatsoever to the actual end result. Not unlike the glossy pictures on the menus of fast food outlets today really. Inside the box were two sachets of ingredients: one the main component, and one the accompanying rice or noodles. With Chinese, you also got a tiny sachet of soy sauce and some dried crispy noodles. These you had to add to hot oil, and they puffed up like miniature Quavers but not cheesy of course. All the ingredients were dried. You just had to add water and stir until cooked, usually about 25 minutes. The only skill required was measuring the water correctly, and we often got that wrong. The meat (and alarmingly the paella prawns) came in tiny cubes. No doubt, it was soya and not meat at all. The list of ingredients took up one whole side of the box, so if I live forever, you'll know why. It's all the preservatives I consumed every weekend. We ate in my room where Sylvia had a small camp bed, balancing our bowls on our knees. We would turn off the lights and watch Peter Cushing or Christopher Lee in the old *Hammer House of Horror* films which were invariably shown late on Saturday night. Afterwards, we lay in our little beds and put the world to rights. Of course, we didn't. We talked about sex. Once Sylvia had passed her test, she used to drive up in her little red mini. I always knew when she arrived because her car engine made such a distinctive noise as she changed gear and rounded the corner on the approach to our house. I definitely corrupted Sylvia. When we first became friends, she was into David Cassidy and Donny Osmond. I soon had her smoking and drinking and rocking out

34

to Bowie and Alice Cooper. Her mother probably liked me about as much as my mother liked Sylvia.

Chapter 4
Romeo and Juliet

When I was fifteen, I started having trouble with my knees. Initially, it was only one knee but soon both were becoming painful and swollen. This went on for ages. I would get better, then for no obvious reason, my knees would become bad again. I was sent to a Consultant Rheumatologist. He initially thought I might have Still's Disease, which, very broadly speaking, is a form of rheumatoid arthritis affecting juveniles. He thought it might be gout but decided I was too young. He said it might just be growth pain. None of the tests carried out were conclusive. It was, it would seem, a medical mystery. I had left school (hurrah). Constant truancy and sickness meant that although I did surprisingly well in my mocks, I failed to sit the final exams, and I left without any qualifications. At the time I wasn't bothered, but of course, now I bitterly regret wasting my education. If only we could turn the clock back and have another go! Also, back then, no one ever questioned why I had gone from a straight-A student to Hampshire's number one truant. Nobody seemed to care, and I certainly didn't, so that was that. Sarah did much better attaining ten 'O' level passes, but then she had never skipped school. I started work in a place called 'The Village' in Portsmouth which was a collection of individual fashion outlets under one roof like an indoor market but trendy. With my love of clothes, I never managed to take home a full wage packet; I always owed most of it by the time I got paid. Items made from cheesecloth were very popular at the time, as were cotton jeans worn low on the hip called 'loons'. I had a pair by French Connection which were dark blue and covered with tiny yellow stars. Platform shoes, of course, were all the rage. I bought some really amazing black leather boots with ultrahigh platforms. Almost every week, I had a new pair of shoes—pity, I couldn't walk for most of the time. Because the job entailed a lot of standing, in the end I had to give it up. I was gutted as I had set my heart on becoming a fashion buyer and maybe having my own boutique one day.

Mother paid for me to attend a private secretarial college, so I could get a sitting down job. Unlike school, I actually loved it. I passed my RSA II typing, Pitman 100 wpm shorthand, English Literature and English Language 'O' Levels and elementary book-keeping! All in the space of a year. Queen were Number One with *Bohemian Rhapsody* and life was good. My first job as a secretary was with a small firm of solicitors, working for the old gentleman who did probate. He was such a nice man. His daughter and I had been in the same class in primary school. He had obviously fathered her later on in life. He was one of those strange people who enjoy swimming in the sea all year round. Still, it obviously kept him healthy—and fertile. He always wore a waistcoat with a gold pocket watch and chain, and when he went out, always carried a large black umbrella.

Also, joy of joy, I had reconnected with Aaron, and I was truly, madly and deeply in love for the first time. I can still remember our getting together so clearly. It was a beautiful summer evening. We had bumped into each other quite by chance and ended up talking and talking until late. He walked me home, a long way through the posh part of Gosport, past beautiful houses with beautiful gardens. The night was still and balmy, the kind of night when you can smell lilies and jasmine and hear the insects chattering. We didn't hurry. We kept stopping to kiss. In fact, progress was slow. We stopped a lot, and he didn't complain, so I must have improved some. This time, when he slipped his hand inside my t-shirt, he seemed more than happy with the size of my boobs—so it was all good. I didn't want that walk to ever end. I often think I would happily trade all my tomorrows for just one yesterday, and I would choose that long ago summer night and the slow walk home in the moonlight with Aaron above everything.

After that, we were officially an item, and we couldn't get enough of each other. He had moved away from Gosport but travelled down every other weekend on his BSA motorbike. In my opinion, nothing will ever beat the sex you have as a teenager. That voyage of exquisite discovery when you fall in love for the first time and have loads of wild energetic sex. My friends laugh at me at me when I say, we flattened a lot of grass. And we did; we were way, way too randy. We tried everything, in every position, in every place; we were insatiable. It was great. We lay for hours together, arms and legs entwined. We studied each other's bodies in minute detail and tried things we liked and things we didn't—and there wasn't a whole lot we didn't. I loved everything about him. I loved his smell. I would nuzzle into his neck and breathe in his scent. I wanted to melt into him completely, to become one with him. I especially loved the thin line of dark hair that ran from his belly button to his groin and the spattering of hairs on his chest. He was slender and lithe, and I adored him. One of the lads, Aaron had gone round with at school, lived in a bungalow just around the corner from my house. He was a strange lad with a mop of bushy hair and a huge nose like my stepfather's brother. Because of his big nose, he was always called 'Trill'. The bungalow belonged to his parents, but he had stayed on in it when they moved to another property. Aaron and I practically lived there. It was really more like a squat where everybody hung out. It was pretty squalid. But we didn't care so long as we could be together. We commandeered one of the bedrooms from which we rarely emerged. When we did come out, it was to take long baths together, slopping water over the side and flooding the floor as we made love. And of course, he serenaded me with Elvis songs and made me laugh, a lot. When he was away, we wrote long X-rated letters to each other. No mobiles phones then of course, and let me tell you, receiving a ten-page letter full of filth courtesy of Royal Mail is far, far better than a smutty text and a picture of your partner's genitals. Unfortunately, mother found and read my diary which described in great detail everything we got up to. I've never been so embarrassed in my life or so mad. Come to think of it, I don't think she had ever been so embarrassed or so mad. The atmosphere between us was very chilly for some time.

Aaron and I dated for a couple of years. Now I look back, we didn't do a whole lot. We were far too busy having sex. When we did come up for air, we played darts at the pub on the corner, a good deal. We were always the only people in there. The landlord was an alcoholic and insulted all his customers, so it was always empty. But mostly we spent our time exploring each other or lying around in the squat drinking beer and listening to music. Gary Numan and Tubeway Army were really popular. *Are Friends Electric* sounded awesome when played at full volume. So did Iggy Pop's *The Passenger*. A few of the people who used the house smoked a bit of weed, usually home grown, but Aaron and I didn't use drugs. We drank of course, and we both smoked cigarettes, John Player Specials for me, roll ups for Aaron. Back then, twenty cigarettes cost about 23p. There was an older guy who stayed at the house who had a bad reputation for dealing drugs. He was very good looking, not unlike a young Cat Stevens with his dark curly hair and short beard. He was always out of his head on something judging by the way he twitched and jerked about. I don't suppose he looks too good nowadays with the amount of chemicals he imbibed, assuming he's even still alive. He had a very young, very pretty girlfriend from an extremely good-moneyed family. She had been privately educated and had a natty little sports car. I bet her parents were well chuffed when she rocked up with him in tow. Young love however can be fickle. I still loved Aaron, but I was becoming tired of him being away all the time. I wanted more. I was fed up with sleeping in beds at other peoples' houses or doing it al fresco. I wanted a boyfriend with a place of his own and maybe a car.

Sylvia had set her sights on a lad she had seen around. She knew which pub he and his mate normally went to and wanted to go there that weekend. She didn't want to go alone and pleaded with me to go with her and if necessary make up a foursome. The problem was Aaron was due to come down. I didn't know how I could tell him not to come, what excuse to make, so Sylvia said she would speak to him. So, like an absolute idiot, I let her make the call, and she told him I didn't want to see him anymore. We had a real falling out over that, and I never really forgave her. It was the beginning of the end of our friendship. I had wanted to put Aaron off for the weekend, not forever. I was ashamed that I hadn't had the guts to explain things to him myself. I convinced myself that he would turn up anyway to speak to me in person, or at least ring, but of course he didn't. He had much too much pride. Or maybe he didn't love me as much as I thought. He might have even been relieved! Perhaps he wanted a girlfriend with a place of her own and a car. I suppose it was nice that our relationship ended on a high. We didn't get to fall out of love with each other and start to bicker. But I will always regret that I was too much of a coward to speak to him. He was probably bonking someone in his home town during the week anyway—would have served me right. In the words of Katy Perry, Aaron will forever be *the one that got away*.

So, I went with my treacherous friend to the pub, and her man's friend was the cutest guy ever. He was very good looking. His face was almost pretty. Aaron was quickly forgotten. It would be a brief relationship, if you can even call it that. I only ever saw him on a Friday night, and we always went to the same pub. Today you would probably describe us as being friends with benefits. I was massively insecure, and it made me overly needy and clingy. I was always asking him if he loved me, which he patently did not. I told myself that as we were having plenty of very satisfactory sex, he must do. After the pub, we would go back to my house and sneak into my bedroom. Mother had always gone to bed by then. He still lived with his parents so we never went there. He hated that he couldn't smoke a joint at mine because of the smell, although, we might have got away with telling mother it was herbal. He loathed Bowie so we played Pink Floyd's *Dark Side of the Moon* and *Wish You Here* to death. In my heart of hearts, I knew he was thinking *Wish I Wasn't Here*, and I was right. He soon found himself a sophisticated and attractive older girl who had her own car and flat. The irony wasn't lost on me. I did meet up with him on a later occasion and gave him a blow job, just to spite her you understand. It only made me feel ever so slightly better.

Sylvia was still hot and heavy with her boyfriend, so I hardly ever saw her. I had arranged to go out with another friend, and we met up at her house. Linda was a big roly-poly girl with teeth like the late Ken Dodd. If I'm truthful, she had definitely been at the back of the queue when the looks were handed out, but she had bags of confidence and was the life and soul of any party. She had an infectious laugh, the sort of person one is happy to be around. She was extremely large but surprisingly feminine and light on her feet. She had a penchant for sexy lingerie and always wore stockings and suspenders, never tights. I only put my suzzies on if I thought there was a chance I might get lucky. She was absolutely crazy about a chap called Danny and talked about him non-stop. How tall he was, how dishy; how she had copped off with him once and had great sex. She was infatuated. In my experience, if you've slept with a bloke, and he hasn't called, it almost certainly means he isn't interested. He probably thinks of you as the local bike. That won't stop him having a good old pedal around; he just won't be jumping on for the long ride. But Linda thought she had a chance. Naturally, I didn't tell her what I really thought. I wanted her to be happy, so I encouraged her, and I told her what she wanted to hear. We jigged about to *Best of My Love* by the Emotions, and as we danced, we got ready. Hair, make-up, perfume, handbags, we were good to go and hot to trot. As the taxi sped towards the John Peel, Linda was keeping everything crossed that tonight she would snag her man.

Chapter 5
Run, Run, Run

The John Peel was a regular haunt of ours. Most Fridays, we would start off in The Seahorse in Gosport for a couple of hours and then go on to The John Peel. They usually had a live band so it was packed, standing room only. Once I was sandwiched up against a bloke, and my bracelet caught in his jumper. As I walked away, it pulled a long thread and half his jumper unravelled. I'm not sure he even noticed; it was that crowded. Probably felt a bit of a draught when he got outside though. It took forever to get served, but it was a happening place, and everyone who was anyone was there. You always came away with fag burns in your clothes and sometimes a bit of hair singed off, but no one cared.

Linda soon spotted her target and homed in. "Isn't he gorgeous?" she mouthed at me. Well, what can I say—he was a hunk. Tall, about 6' 2", well built, not fat but muscular. He had light brown hair, shoulder length, maybe slightly shorter and a beard. Not Captain Birdseye but certainly more than stubble. He had very blue eyes and long dark eyelashes. Picture an Anglicised Jesus but with a ripped body and that was what he looked like. As for me, I was petite, and I scrubbed up well. I had a massive inferiority complex so I never thought of myself as pretty or even attractive. I was often told I looked like a young Cher, in her 'I Got You Babe' era, or sometimes Barbra Streisand. I think it was the nose. It's sad that when we are young, is when we feel most insecure about our looks. It's only when we get old and look back we realise just what we had, the beauty of youth. I remember as a teenager seeing a film of Queen Elizabeth's wedding and thinking she was a bit of a dog. Now, when I see that film, I think how beautiful she was. And you were Ma'am. Anyway, my eyes locked with Danny's, and the chemistry was palpable. We both fancied each other something rotten. Linda didn't notice. She twittered away, trying to flirt with Danny and not seeing what was happening in front of her eyes. It was all rather awkward. Of course, the music was so loud, we couldn't really make conversation. We just shouted to each other. Danny stooping low so I could holler in his ear. Finally, the night came to an end, and Linda and I got a taxi home. This, dear reader, is when you are going to be thoroughly ashamed of me. What I did was sly, sneaky and altogether horrible. A soon as the taxi had dropped Linda off I doubled back in it to meet up with Danny. I did feel bad (a little bit), but I would get my comeuppance. As the saying goes, you reap what you sow, and Linda, you had a very, very lucky escape.

We went back to his house. He lived with his mum, dad and two sisters who were unidentical twins in a large council house in what was quite a rough area. It certainly was an eye-opener for me. I had never even met anyone from a council house before. Inside, the lounge looked just the Trotter's front room in *Only Fools and Horses*. His mum and dad were in bed so we went straight up to his bedroom. It was obvious he liked wacky backy. There were a couple of bongs on a low pine shelf and an open box full of skinning up paraphernalia, a bit of a giveaway. We didn't have sex. I slept with him in his bed, but we only kissed and cuddled. I would really like to tell you that I wouldn't have sex with a man on the first night, but that would be a lie. I didn't have sex with him because I had my period. Believe me, I wanted to. If I had been at the end of my period, maybe I would have done. Who am I trying to kid? I would have jumped his bones. So we cuddled, and we chatted, and we liked each other a lot. He had noticeable stammer, but I found that quite endearing. He told me it had been worse as a child, and he had seen a speech therapist who taught him the technique of making a kind of clicking sound before each word. We were woken in the morning by a loud knock, and a cheery face complete with grey stubble and nicotine-stained teeth appeared round the door. "All right, love (large wink)—Want a cuppa? Fuck me, she's a bit of all right—you done well for yourself there son." (Another large wink). So there I was, just woken up, naked as a jay-bird, in a strange bed with a man I had only recently met, clutching a thin sheet to cover my modesty being introduced to his father.

Luckily, he didn't attempt to shake my hand. Apparently, it was absolutely fine, one might even say expected, for Danny to have a girl stay the night, but if either of the twins (who were nineteen at the time) had even thought about inviting a man back, there would have been murder, literally. Talk about double standards.

I really liked Danny. I liked his family. I liked the way they swore and ribbed each other, their easy ways. Down in the kitchen, his mum, Val, was frying bacon. Dave was buttering toast with Stork margarine. My mother would only ever use Stork for baking, certainly not for toast, only ever butter. Val was wearing a pale pink nylon negligee with a great many frills. It was cut low at the neck, exposing a large expanse of wrinkly bosom. She was extremely tall and had jet black hair back-combed into a large beehive, slightly askew at this time in the morning. Her eyebrows were drawn on in black kohl eye pencil. She had a cigarette in her mouth which bobbed up and down as she talked, the long tip of ash threatening at any moment to fall onto the bacon. Dave was in his vest which was none too clean and had a gold sovereign ring on almost every finger. They both had the hacking coughs of lifelong smokers evident each time they laughed, but they were incredibly friendly. They swore like navvies. My parents would never had said the 'F' word. I'm pretty sure my mother wouldn't have even known it. She would say 'Damn' quite a lot and occasionally 'Bloody'. Then you knew she was seriously angry. I think from all the winks and nudges, Dave and Val thought I was a bit of a posh bird and quite a catch for their son. They certainly treated me like a duchess.

Danny told me he was a civil engineer. How gullible was I? You need some serious qualifications to be a civil engineer. I know that now, but back then, for a short while, I believed him. He was actually a labourer. He wasn't educated; I'm not even sure if he could read and write. If he could, it wasn't very well. He told me he had money in the bank, ready for a deposit on a house. Not true, no one in the family had so much as set foot in a bank—unless it was to do a reccy. He told me his Mercedes was in the garage being fixed, when he had no car. However, all this was for the future. He was so charming, and I was falling for him. He had a huge reputation for fighting. In particular, people were scared of him and his older brother. The whole family were notorious, like a down-market version of the Krays. Danny had been in prison a couple of times for GBH and ABH, and both his older brothers had done quite long stretches. I've always found the bad boys attractive. In the 1991 film *Robin Hood Prince of Thieves,* it wasn't Kevin Costner I couldn't take my eyes off; it was the Sheriff of Nottingham played by the wonderful Alan Rickman. He was also hot as baddie Hans Gruber in *Die Hard.* To my mind, the Bond villains are usually more attractive than Bond. Christopher Walken as Max Zorin in *View to a Kill* is a good example. Not sure about Ernst Blofeld though. I find Vladimir Putin strangely attractive, and if you believe all you read, he certainly seems to get plenty of action, so clearly, I'm not alone. I love a Russian accent. If I was married to Steve Carell, I would make him speak in like Felonius Gru all the time and especially in bed.

There were eight boys in Danny's family, all roughly a year apart, then a gap of two years before the twins were born. Val must have been permanently pregnant. Money was tight, and often there was only enough for Dave to have a hot meal. The kids made do with bread and margarine, or bread and milk (which was often watered down). In our family, bread and milk was what you put out at night for the hedgehogs. I should stress that this was in complete ignorance. Hedgehogs should never be given bread and milk, it can make them very ill or even kill them. Best save it for your children. Danny said the kids would take it in turns to have any morsel left on their father's plate. My mother would always have fed us before my stepfather no matter how tight the money was. Lucky would have been fed before my stepfather. Once, Danny was invited by a school friend for tea, and they had a mixed grill, chops, sausages, bacon and kidneys, the works. He said it was one of the best meals he had ever eaten. When he had the same friend back to his, Val made them dumplings on jam.

Dave would frequently take his belt to the boys. Sometimes he would whack them with the buckle end. One time when Danny was naughty, his dad tied him to a lamp-post and left him there until nearly midnight. When the landlord of their local banned one of the boys over what Val considered a triviality, she stormed into the bar, grabbed a pool cue and started smashing all the glasses. She said it was to give the landlord something to really ban the family for. Val was also fond of recounting the story of when Danny had come home drunk from a fancy dress party in the wee small hours and collapsed in the garden. Early next morning, the milkman knocked the door and asked if Val knew there was a womble lying on her front lawn. I had never met people like these, and I honestly don't think they had met anyone like me. I basked in their admiration when I should have run for the hills—fast.

Danny's friends made a great fuss of me. I was told many times that I was the best girl Danny had ever gone out with, and I think that was probably true. Looking back, I was certainly the stupidest! I loved his mates; they were so complimentary, it was hard not to. We socialised with them all the time. They all lived in council houses or flats. One couple I particularly liked were called Taff and Anna. I'm not sure why he was called Taff, I don't think he was Welsh. They were older than Danny and had been together for donkey's years. Taff made no attempt to hide the fact that he thought I was lovely. Even Danny teased him about it, and Anna just laughed. He always called me a 'little beauty'. Anna was the tiniest woman I have ever seen; she was like a small child. They were both really, really thin. I don't think they ate, which was surprising considering the amount of dope they both smoked. And there was a whole lotta dope smoking going on. We were all permanently stoned and of course that created a great deal of laughter. Every little thing seems funny when you smoke marijuana. I soon learnt how to roll a joint. I could still do it now; it's on my resume as a useful skill. The dope then was much less potent than it is now. It could still make you feel paranoid but not nearly so much as the skunk people smoke today. I never used a bong or a pipe—too strong. I didn't like the feeling of being really stoned so in the main I partook quite moderately and, compared to the others, was a bit of a lightweight. Danny introduced me to amphetamine otherwise known as speed, which was usually in the form of little bright blue pills or 'blues'. I loved taking speed. It made you feel so alive. It didn't make your eyes red like cannabis but large and limpid with dilated pupils. And unlike cannabis, you didn't want to eat the entire contents of the fridge in one sitting as it killed your appetite. This made it very popular with the girls. Mother once told me that when she was touring as a skater, some of the girls used to take pills to kill their appetites and keep them slim.

Now there's a thought to conjure with, perhaps my mother wasn't so innocent. Perhaps she liked a bit of whizz back in the day. The downside of speed was that you didn't sleep and that was horrible. Also, it could be highly addictive. After a while, we started to rely on it to have a good time. I tried cocaine on a couple of occasions. I never snorted anything; it just doesn't appeal, despite the fact that I've got a big nose and would probably have been a natural. So I swallowed my little bit of coke wrapped in a Rizla cigarette paper. I tried it twice, but got nothing from it so I never had it again. LSD and magic mushrooms were both popular. I never tried either and wasn't even remotely tempted. I was way too scared of having a bad experience or to use the vernacular a 'bad trip'. One well-known character was regularly seen shuffling and lurching around Gosport reminiscent of a zombie, his eyes vacant and staring. The story was that as a young man, he had taken one too many hallucinogenic drugs. It was certainly enough to put me off.

We spent many happy evenings, stoned out of our tiny minds, listening to the Beatles, The Rolling Stones, Genesis, Santana, Led Zeppelin, Tom Petty, Eric Clapton and Van Morrison; bands I love to this day. In between listening to music and often during, Danny and I had an awful lot of steamy sex. He could be rather rough, but I'm not averse to being thrown about the bedroom when I'm in the mood so I didn't object. All part of life's rich tapestry. In those days, we all listened to the same music. New albums were hugely anticipated. When *Rumours* was released, we all rushed out to buy it. Walk along any road, and you would hear Fleetwood Mac blaring from somebody's open window. Meat Loaf's *Bat Out of Hell* was another album that everybody bought and Eric Clapton's *Slowhand*. The same went for TV. There were only three channels, and we all watched the same programmes. The next day, it would be, "Did you see *'The Rise and Fall of Reginald Perrin'* last night?" We would then go through the entire script verbatim, repeating the one-liners as if the person with whom we were talking hadn't just said they had watched it. At Christmas, practically the whole country watched the unsurpassable Morecambe & Wise. Eric and Ernie dressed as Roman centurions in 'a play what Ernie wrote'—"Have you got the scrolls?"

"No, I always walk like this"—still makes me laugh. Now, you can never discuss anything. Everyone listens to different music and watches different channels on TV. I think it's rather sad. We are all gradually isolating ourselves.

With the exception of my sister, my family loved Danny. He could be incredibly sweet and charming when he wanted to. Sarah wasn't impressed because Danny was thick and she finds lack of intellect a huge turn-off. The first time he came to our house and tried to sit down, a chorus of voices cried, "That's Lucky's chair," so he had to abide by the house rules, and even he wasn't hard enough to mess with Lucky. We had been dating for three months when we had the bright idea to get married. My mother was thrilled, his parents were thrilled, his friends were thrilled. Nobody, least of all me, thought, *Isn't this a bit soon? Do you really know each other?* Hindsight is a wonderful thing; I was walking into a perfect storm. I was aware by then that he was a little economical with the truth. His friends called him 'Jackanory' because he told such good stories, but of course no one called him that to his face. The red flags were waving, but I didn't heed the warning. I thought he was 'the one' and I loved him. It goes without saying that I never got an engagement ring.

I was nineteen years old when we married on a cold January morning. Danny was twenty-five. The wedding was pretty awful. I wore black corduroy trousers and a jumper with a string of pearls just to show that I had made the effort. I had recently had a 'shaggy' perm, and my red hair looked pretty awesome if I say so myself. I didn't want a wedding dress. The only wedding dresses available back then made you look like a large walking meringue. Not like now, the dresses are stunning, and I wouldn't hesitate to wear one should I ever be asked, which isn't very likely. Danny wore a nice suit and looked very handsome. What with being nervous and his stutter, he had a lot of trouble with the words 'lawful impediment' and was stuck for ages, like a record with a bad scratch. If the Registrar hadn't waved him on, I think we would still be there. When it came to the marriage certificate, he actually put himself down as 'civil engineer'. One of the witnesses commented, "He's not an engineer, and he's never been bloody civil," which caused a good deal of mirth. Afterwards the reception, all arranged by Danny's dad was held at the local RNLI Club. No transport was laid on for the guests;

they came from the Register Office on a Hants & Dorset double-decker. At the reception, Taff goosed Sarah and called her 'a little beauty'. I don't think he ever realised just how close he came to death that day. She was not amused. Lidl's did the catering. A limp piece of lettuce, half an overripe tomato, a slice of economy ham and two or three tinned potatoes. Yes, tinned potatoes, and they were like bullets. I bet your mouth is watering as you read. Of course, there was super-super-economy salad cream to moisten thing ups. Sorry, I'm talking it down, we had a hard-boiled egg as well. I didn't dare look at my sister.

Well, that was my big day. Unsurprisingly, there was no cake, and there was no honeymoon either. Unless you count moving in with my family until we found a place of our own. Still, we were young and in love, and the future looked bright.

Chapter 6
Truth No. 2

After about a month, we found a flat to rent. We were really pleased to be leaving my mother's. It had been difficult living there. For a start, we had to squeeze into a single bed which was terribly hot and uncomfortable. One night, Danny got up to go to the loo and bumped into my mother. As he always slept nude, I'm not sure who was more surprised, him or my mother, but I'm guessing my mother. The new flat consisted of the bottom half of a big house for £80 a month, which was very reasonable. The living room was huge and had a lovely open fireplace. There was also a beautiful tile and black marble fireplace in the large bedroom. It was furnished, so perfect in every way. We met the landlord, and of course Danny laid it on with a trowel. How hard working he was, how he hoped shortly to be buying our own house and how much he earned. I was beginning to feel embarrassed by all his embellishments, but the poor landlord was duped. From the day we moved in until the day we left eighteen months later, I don't think he was paid any rent, and he was either too scared to press it or knew it would be futile. On the rare occasions when he did come round, Danny would send me to the door to make excuses. I think the landlord genuinely felt sorry for me. He must have thrown the party of all parties when we did eventually leave.

I got a job as a Playboy bunny. Sarah and I both went for the interview. Old clever clogs immediately got taken on as a trainee croupier, but I failed the maths and was offered the job of lobby bunny—receptionist in other words. We went to be fitted for our costumes which were made to measure. I had three. One was red with gold trim, one was green satin, and one was black velvet with silver trim—that was my favourite. We wore two pairs of tights, a dark tan pair first and then over the top a pair of very sheer black. They were specially made with no gussets, like those worn by dancers, as the costumes were cut so high over the hips. For the same reason, we didn't wear knickers. The costumes were heavily boned or wired to be more precise and were extremely tight, like a corset. There was a pocket in each bra cup which we packed with toilet roll and then sat our boobs on top. This greatly enhanced your bosom and gave the appearance that you were spilling out over the top of the costume. At first, I needed help fastening and unfastening the hooks at the back, but I soon got the hang of doing it myself. The large fluffy white tail was attached by four giant poppers. We had a little soft white collar with a black clip-on bow tie and matching white cuffs fastened with silver and black enamel cufflinks, sporting the Playboy logo. The ears were in the same colour as the costume and wired so they stood to attention. They were attached to your head by a rigid hairband held in place with hairgrips. The outfit was completed by a name badge also with the Playboy logo which was pinned onto a black satin rosette and attached to your hip. A lot of the girls didn't use their real names but plumped for something more exotic, like Sabrina or Anastasia, but I used my real name. I did toy with the idea of being called Stella as it's my favourite name. Also, it means star which is neat, and I'm very fond of lager. Finally, we wore high black leather court shoes, especially made for Playboy. No one was allowed to start their shift until they had been inspected by the Bunny Mother and passed muster. She checked our hair, make-up, nail varnish and overall appearance. Shifts were from 7pm–2am or 9pm–4am. It was great fun and wearing the costume made you feel incredibly sexy.

My sister married another croupier. After only a short time together, she went to work for Playboy in Nassau. Her new husband remained at the casino in Portsmouth where I was also working. It wasn't long before he was openly having an affair with one of the girls at the club, which was rather awkward for me. Later, I found out that Sarah knew all about his philandering. She was having such a good time in the Bahamas; she really wasn't bothered. I was able to get a lift into work and home again from the club DJ who lived in Gosport. If it hadn't been for him, I would have had to get a taxi each night as Playboy only paid for transport to the city limits at the end of each shift. Eventually, the DJ moved on, and I had to leave. I was struggling anyway. We were seated in our little lobby reception, but I was still in pain a lot of the time. When I did have to walk around, it was tough, the heels were so high. No one wants to see a limping bunny. Not long after, Playboy lost their gaming licence, and the casino closed. When I left, I kept my green satin costume which I eventually sold on eBay. I regret now that I parted with my Playboy name badge, it would have been a nice memento. Anyway, to whoever bought the costume, I hope you're having fun! As well as my knees, my hands and wrists were now giving me trouble. I had begun a new job working for a solicitor at their office in Gosport. I was secretary to the conveyancer Tom. At twenty-eight, he was young and seemed really nice. I shared an office with a girl called Dawn who worked for the matrimonial lawyer. We were to become firm friends.

Things at home were not so good. We were having huge rows and it was becoming obvious that Danny was an aggressive bully. He never paid any bills. He earned reasonable money as a labourer but spent it all on clothes for himself, booze and drugs. Everything we had was stolen. Our TV was nicked. It was carried in under cover of darkness wrapped in a bedspread (also nicked). Of course, we never had a licence. Our freezer was nicked, and our cooker was nicked. One night, he and his mates pinched the entire contents of a pub's beer garden, literally all the wooden tables and benches were loaded into a van and driven away. He gave my mother one of the tables which she treasured for years. We had two of the smaller ones in our front room. We also had a full set of pub optics (nicked) and the bottles of spirits to go with them (nicked). He drove a real old banger of a car which couldn't have been roadworthy. The exhaust emitted vast clouds of black smoke and fumes. The car was forever breaking down, in which case, he would hijack some poor passerby to give him a push. If there was no one around, and at 6 am this was often the case, he would walk back to the flat and get me up to help. He had never had a driving lesson let alone taken a test so had no licence, no MOT and no insurance. Didn't bother him in the slightest. A stream of wasters arrived at all hours of the night and day to buy and sell drugs. If we weren't in, they would sit on the wall at the front of the house and wait. You could tell just by the look of them that they were drug addicts.

At the grand old age of seventeen, Lucky died. He had remained feisty to the end. Shortly before he died, he scratched a little lad who tried to stroke him. The boy's mother knocked my mother's door and had a right go at her. Danny knew how I loved cats. He brought home a black and white kitten who we christened Nobby. He was a timid little thing, and because he was so nervous, Danny started to scare him at every opportunity. It got to the stage that just the sound of Danny approaching would send Nobby into a blind panic. He would try to get into the kitchen cupboard skidding across the floor spraying urine and defecating as he fled. It was truly horrible to witness. When Danny was due home, I would take Nobby into the bathroom and keep him out of the way to give Danny time to put the TV on and settle in the front room. Our flat was on a busy main road, and Nobby was run over and killed when he was less than a year old. He probably committed suicide.

Because we had open fires and never enough money for the electric meter, Danny took to breaking up the landlord's wooden furniture to burn. Once the furniture had been exhausted, he started dismantling the shed, and once that had gone, the garden fence. By the time we moved out, there was barely a scrap of wood left on the premises. The damage inside was also extensive. He had put his fist through every door. All the interior door glass was smashed. God knows what the neighbours thought. I've got a smart mouth, and I wouldn't go down without a fight. Some of our rows were epic, but he always cowed me in the end. Once he had smashed his way into the bedroom, broken the full length mirror and was hurling crockery at the wall above my head. I screamed that I was calling the police. "You want the fucking police?" he hollered, "I'll get the fucking police," and he grabbed up the phone and called the fucking police.

When they arrived, they merely asked at the door if I was OK, and of course I said, "Yes," so they left. Another time, he booted our Sunday roast, a large leg of pork out into the main road. He did the same thing with our wicker cat-carrying basket (it was empty, I hasten to add). He booted that into the road, and amazingly a passing car stopped, grabbed it up and drove off. What are the chances?

My illness had at long last been diagnosed. I had Systemic Lupus Erythematosis, otherwise known as SLE or Lupus. It's one of the many auto-immune illnesses where the immune system attacks itself. Then it was rarely heard of, but now it is much more widely known. I was becoming very ill, especially in the evenings. My fingers and hands would swell so much they didn't resemble hands anymore. I had terrible joint pain pretty much all over, very much like rheumatoid arthritis. I couldn't perform my ablutions at bedtime. I couldn't get my clothes off or on. Sometimes my jaw was affected, and I couldn't open my mouth. The pain in the centre of my hands was dreadful. I used to imagine it was exactly what having nails driven through your hands during crucifixion must have felt like. The pain and stiffness made me feel old and unattractive, and Danny called me that, frequently. During the daytime, I was usually fine. Occasionally, I had a flare-up, but it was mainly in the evening, and it was every evening. Nobody knew how poorly I was. I was living a horrible double life, and it would continue for the next 30 years.

Some good news at last! Danny got a job away labouring in London and would be gone all week. Honestly, it was bliss, real bliss. I could watch what I wanted on TV. I could eat what I wanted when I wanted. There were no rows. I loved it. Of course, the downside was that he came home on a Friday. Usually he would go out, but I knew he would want sex when he came back, and I dreaded it. Danny wanted sex all the time. I became adept at faking it. Sometimes he would go on for what seemed like hours, and I would be praying for him to hurry up and finish. Often, by the end of a long session, I had given up even trying to pretend I was enjoying it, and I lay there like a wrung out rag. I know I did an awful lot of laying back and thinking of Britain. If Danny noticed my lack of enthusiasm, he never commented. I don't think it particularly bothered him that I wasn't actively participating so long as he got his end away. I can't tell you how happy I was when Sunday came around, and I could wave him off for another week.

One time when Danny was away, a friend of ours called John popped round. John and I had been flirting with each other for ages (not when Danny was looking of course). He was really hot. There was a lot of chemistry and sexual tension between us. I think we would both have liked an opportunity to rip each other's clothes off. Sometimes you can just tell that a man would be really good in bed. He was great company too, bright and quick witted. We gelled. That particular night, there was a party, and we decided to go. I don't think there was much doubt in either of our minds what the outcome would be. Happy Days! We set off, and as we walked, our hands kept brushing sending thrills through me like tiny electric shocks. We kissed a few times. Lovely, long deep kisses; I could have eaten him up. We arrived at the party, and suddenly we were very nervous. The enormity of what we were about to do hit us both. So many people there knew Danny, and someone would have taken great delight in telling him they had seen us together. We completely lost our nerve. Our ardour cooled quicker than if someone had doused us with ice water. We both knew that Danny would have killed us. We went home separately, although, we did continue to flirt if ever we met up after that. I still kick myself that we didn't at least have a quickie in the bushes, or at the very least a knee-trembler. I must have been having an off day.

A few years later, I heard that John had drowned in a tragic accident.

Chapter 7
Blue Turk

Danny and I bought a house. It was a bit like when couples decide to have a baby, or get a dog to cement their failing relationship. Never works, but they try. Danny was full of promises not to drink so much, not to be violent, to be more responsible with money, to take less drugs. I don't think I really believed him, but I wanted to. He kept pestering me to try for a baby, and I would have loved one but not with him. I didn't want his genes for my child, and I didn't want to be tied to him forever through a child. And there was the violence. Of course, I didn't voice these thoughts. We still had some good times. We went to some great concerts—Genesis, Bruce Springstein, Peter Frampton, Supertramp, Lou Reed, Joe Jackson, The Sensational Alex Harvey Band, Graham Parker and Nils Lofgren to name a few. A whole group of us went to a one-day festival where The Who were headlining. As the support act were warming up for The Who, a fight broke out. I'm not sure who started it, but I would bet money that it was one of our lot. It was very frightening; the crowd parted like the Red Sea as everyone scrambled to get out of the way. The women were desperately trying to pull their men away as punches were thrown. I remember seeing one young man on the ground, and as he tried to protect himself, Taff swung his foot back and kicked him in the head two or three times. After that, I never felt the same about Taff. I had thought he was so nice. Now I saw him for what he was, a violent thug. It was a sobering experience, and it ruined the whole concert for me. We did have a nice camping holiday in Wales with another couple, although, it rained the whole time, and it was cold. We arrived in the afternoon and found a remote spot by a stream to pitch our tents. It was probably on private land, but a little thing like that wouldn't have worried us. Off we went to the nearest pub for the evening, and of course when we returned, it was pitch black. No one had thought to take a torch. We stumbled about, trying to see by the flame of a Bic lighter but it was no good. We couldn't find the tent. We didn't even know if we were in the right field. We had to walk all the way back which was quite a long way and sleep in the car.

The new house was an Edwardian mid-terrace. My boss did the conveyancing free of charge and helped us arrange the mortgage. We didn't have a deposit, but some Building Societies were granting 100% mortgages so we took advantage of this. The house had been modernised with a new kitchen and bathroom extension. The bathroom suite was avocado green. Pretty much everyone's bathroom suite back then was avocado green; it was very much in vogue. Coloured suites in general were popular, dark chocolate brown, burgundy and for the seriously trendy, black. People were chucking out their boring white bathtubs en masse. Cast iron roll-top baths with their small ornate feet piled up in tips and scrapyards all over the country; they had no place in the modern home. Artex ceilings were another trend. People everywhere tore down their beautiful flat ceilings and applied Artex. This allowed texture to be added to the plaster, in evermore elaborate patterns. New builds always had Artex ceilings. Now these ceilings seem truly horrible, but we all seemed to like them back then. There were two downstairs reception rooms separated by a staircase and two bedrooms off. Danny built two absolutely beautiful fireplaces one in each of the downstairs rooms. All the bricks were stolen from the site where he worked, as was the cement mixer. Danny said the site foreman allowed for this. "Wastage," he called it—no wonder brickwork is so expensive. I'm not sure if a missing cement mixer counts as wastage, but anything's possible. We had a nice new TV (nicked), a microwave (nicked) and a washing machine (fell off the back of a lorry). Security at Carpetland must have been tight, as we only had bare floorboards. There was no central heating. The kitchen and bathroom extension faced north and was particularly chilly. We lived in the middle room where we had a second-hand sofa which we were paying for on tick and while the mortar in the fireplaces was drying out, a three bar electric fire. After a couple of months, Danny stopped paying for the sofa.

My feelings for Danny had cooled. In fact, they were stone cold dead. When we first met, I shivered with delight when he touched me; now I just shivered. I spent most of the time slapping him away. He had no manners. If I was having a bath, he would saunter in, sit on the toilet and have a crap. I actually think he waited until I was having a bath. He thought it was hilarious. He rarely bothered to pull the chain after using the loo, never if it was just a pee. He farted and belched constantly. He had some truly horrible expressions. He referred to my time of the month as being 'on the blob'. Whenever he wanted a cup of tea or a beer, he would say, "I'm as dry as a nun's cunt." I mean honestly! He continued to have tantrums and smash things up. He couldn't go to the pub without getting absolutely wasted. After a skinful, he frequently wet the bed. A couple of times, he got up and pissed in the wardrobe. We were falling more and more into debt. There was a pub at the end of our terrace, so he was there most nights, spending money we didn't have. He would stagger home at closing time, usually with two or three hangers on and put the stereo on so loudly, the house would shake. We had the police round all the time because of the noise. They were always really nice. They knew Danny well, and I honestly think they thought he was a lovable rogue—although they always seemed to turn up mob-handed just in case. Most people did like Danny, but then, they weren't married to him.

In the morning, inevitably, we would row. I love plants and had them all over the house. A big glossy rubber plant, a cheese plant, African violets the ubiquitous spider plant. He booted every single one into the back alley, pots and all; nothing was left. I remember looking at my rubber plant lying broken in the dirt; it's white china pot in pieces; it looked really sad. He smashed a valuable jardinière that used to be my nan's and which he knew I treasured. He was genuinely sorry for that afterwards, only because he knew it had value, but it was too late, the damage was done metaphorically and physically. He used to sit on me, pinning my arms and let long strings of drool fall from his mouth onto my face, or he would spit on me again and again until my face was wet with saliva. Once he held me up against the living room door and stabbed a knife all around my head, like some warped parody of a knife throwing act. He would put his face right up in mine and suddenly make as if to headbutt me, just stopping short. Another favourite was hurling his dinner against the wall. He would slap me, but he never punched. We had two more cats by then, kittens he had brought home, and he would say, "If one of the cats comes in now, I'll kill it." I would pray to God, "Please, please don't let either of the cats come in." They never did; they could hear the pandemonium and stayed away. We had some goldfish in a little plastic aquarium, and he picked that up and launched it. On quite a few occasions I ran out into night wearing just a pair of pyjamas with my coat on top.

When I was ill and stiff in the evenings, he would call me 'hag' and 'crippled cunt'. He couldn't understand why I didn't want to smoke dope or take speed anymore. I told him it made my illness worse, and I was no longer enjoying it, but he just thought I was a big fat party pooper. He would frequently threaten that if I left him, he would find me wherever I went and would scar me so badly that nobody would want me. I don't think it dawned on him that he had already scarred me—mentally. I realise that, to a lot of people who are battered physically on a regular basis, what I went through might not seem that bad, but I was so scared of him. Really, really scared. His face would contort with rage and morph into the face of a demon, like watching Dr Jekyll become Mr Hyde. My insides would turn to water when I knew he was about to kick off. My nerves were completely shredded. I am convinced that the only reason he didn't punch me was that I was so tiny compared to him and everybody would know what he was. Image was very important to Danny. Sometimes, I thought a punch would be preferable to the verbal abuse, the constant threats and the house being left like a tornado had hit it.

I could almost certainly have obtained an injunction to have him removed from the house and prevented from returning. Working for a solicitor, it would have been easy. However, I knew that involving the police and ultimately the courts would be like a red rag to a bull, and it would be a red rag the size of a bed sheet. Danny would not have taken it well, and what's more, he wouldn't have taken any notice. And how fast could the police get to the house in an emergency? They would have had to have been parked up outside to offer any protection. In my mind, an injunction wasn't an option. I used to fantasise all the time about how I could kill him. I thought of drugging him or smothering him when he was drunk. I thought of making a risotto using toadstools (I thought they were mushrooms Your Honour) with a generous sprinkling of yew berries for a garnish. Or slipping a couple of oleander leaves into his sandwiches. If I was out walking, I would find myself scanning the verges for deadly nightshade and hemlock. I loathed him. I couldn't help thinking it might have been nice to live in the Victorian era. You could poison your enemies with impunity. Anybody who upset you, a quick trip to the chemist for a bottle of arsenic or strychnine, invite them round for tea, job done. In an age with no fingerprinting or forensics, one wonders how many murderers did get away with it. Of course if you did get caught, you would surely hang, but I'd say it was a risk worth taking.

When Danny had calmed down, the apologies would come. The promises that it would never, ever happen again. How much he loved me. How he couldn't live without me. And he would wheedle for sex. I couldn't bear him touching me. I never slept with him anymore. For once, I wished he had managed to nick a spare bed as I would have been in it. The last couple of times we did have sex, I turned my face away so he couldn't kiss me and clamped my hands over my nipples so he couldn't touch me there. I felt like I was being raped which in a way I was. I knew I couldn't go on.

It didn't help that I was beginning to have feelings for my boss.

Chapter 8
Do You Want to Know a Secret?

My relationship with Tom was a slow burner. I had been his secretary for a while, and we got on very well. Everyone in the office knew how bad things were at home. I had to talk to someone. I don't think Tom could believe how I could have fallen for somebody like Danny; I didn't believe it myself anymore. Those early days when I thought he was wonderful were a distant memory. Tom never asked me why I didn't leave, but I'm pretty sure he must have thought it. Dawn however, who was dating a rather cute estate agent, never left off telling me I should get out. Whenever Tom ventured into the main office, we would all laugh and chat, but if I had to go into his room to do the filing for example, I would be tongue-tied and shy, and he would become suddenly engrossed in a letter, or a file. I thought him very handsome, in a public schoolboy sort of way.

At 6'3" Tom was slightly taller than Danny. He was about the same weight but didn't appear as muscular. Danny's work as a labourer kept him in good shape. He couldn't have been healthy though, with all the smoking, drinking and drug taking, whereas Tom was extremely fit. He had almost black hair, very thick, cut short with a side parting and very pale skin. He had a moustache, and his eyes were hazel. He reminded me of a young Dustin Hoffman, especially the eyes. He was incredibly awkward around women. From the age of seven until he took his 'A' levels, he had been to an all boys' boarding school in Devon. I can't imagine sending a little seven-year-old off to school only seeing them in the holidays, but Tom was firmly in favour of it, said it was character building. He did concede however that on the few occasions when the girls from the nearby private school were invited for a dance, it was all rather difficult. There were a lot of red-faced wall-flowers and awkward shuffling of feet. I suspect the girls found it quite embarrassing as well.

Tom was so different to Danny. He wore a suit and tie to work; he was clean, and he smelt really, really good. He didn't smoke; he was intelligent, and he never swore or told vulgar jokes. I couldn't help but compare them, and Danny was sadly wanting. When I got home, I would notice how old Danny was starting to look, especially when he first got in from work and was covered in concrete dust. His skin was coarse and weathered from working outside; his hands calloused and dirty. Tom's hands looked soft with long tapering fingers on the back of which were just a few springy black hairs. His nails were short and neat. I used to imagine those hands doing all sorts of things to me. They were very sexy. He was very sexy, and he was beginning to fill my every waking thought.

Every lunchtime, he would join me and Dawn in our room, and we would push our typewriters back and have a race to see who could complete the Sun crossword first. I was never beaten, and it drove him mad. He was fiercely competitive. Just to be clear, I am talking the Sun crossword, so it wasn't exactly difficult, but I loved beating him. I really did. I'm sure it was my prowess with the Sun crossword that first made Tom look at me in a different light. At the time, he was seeing a solicitor who worked for another firm and with whom he regularly played squash. Her name was Janice. By all accounts, she was pretty keen, but I got the impression that so far as Tom was concerned, it was more casual. There was an older lady called Margery who worked as a legal executive in the office, and she definitely had in mind her daughter for the future Mrs Tom. Tom had once taken the daughter to a firm's 'do' but wasn't enamoured. The daughter however really had the hots for him and Margery was on a mission to get them together and ultimately down the aisle. I suspect she may have even bought the hat. She never missed an opportunity to mention that her daughter was single and to relate countless anecdotes about her whenever Tom was around. The other lawyer in the office was Mr Walsingham. Dawn was his secretary. He was also a senior partner in the firm and a District Judge. He was a very nice man indeed, but I was completely in awe of him.

I couldn't help noticing that as is usually the case in the work place, the office plants looked tired and neglected. Although I hadn't long started the job, I thought it would create a good impression if my green fingers were to work their magic. Next day, I took some plant food and a small watering can into work with me. When I had a spare minute, I politely knocked Mr Walsingham's door and sidled in, watering can full and at the ready. Mr Walsingham was sat behind an enormous mahogany desk, reading a broadsheet newspaper. You wouldn't have caught him doing the Sun crossword. He was wearing his usual immaculate pin-striped suit and had little half-lens gold-rimmed glasses perched on his nose over which he peered as he read. The four filing cabinets in his room were also mahogany to match the desk. The cabinets in the rest of the office were all metal, so his were rather posh. On top of one, barely clinging to life, was an Aspidistra. I cleared away some of the dead leaves and poured a generous glug of water into the large pot. Because the compost was bone dry, the water ran straight through. I watched in absolute horror as it flooded over the drip tray and cascaded down the front and sides of the cabinet like a waterfall. I tried desperately to use the sleeves of my jumper to stem the torrent and absorb the small lake which had formed on top of the cabinet. All this in total silence but for the occasional sound of a broadsheet page turning and the faint drip of water (and my sweat) as it fell onto the Axminster carpet. By then, both my sleeves were soaking, and I was trying to use the bottom of my skirt as a mop. After what seemed like an age, I heard a polite little cough, and Mr Walsingham said, "I think there are some paper towels in reception, why don't you get some of those."

Tom said he had an even worse experience. When he joined the firm as an articled clerk, the Walsinghams threw a black tie party at their home to welcome the new intake of trainees. All the solicitors from across the firm attended, together with their partners. Apart from Mr Walsingham's children, Tom said he was the only person without a date. The house was palatial, with a games room and large indoor heated swimming pool. Because Tom was on his own and somewhat immature, he ended up challenging one of the Walsingham children to a game of table tennis. Tom was never going to let a fifteen-year-old beat him and was playing to win. Whilst executing a rather nifty backhand, he hit the table taking out a large chip and breaking the handle off the bat. Apologies made and game abandoned, he straightened his dickie bow and headed in to get some food. There was a large wheel of cheddar on a fine bone china plate and Tom, being fond of cheese, thought he would have a slice. He managed to get the knife stuck, and as he applied pressure, the knife suddenly went right through the cheese and broke the plate underneath clean in half. Later on, in the drawing room Tom backed into a freestanding corner cabinet, rocking it against the wall and causing all the ornaments to rattle alarmingly. Luckily, this time nothing broke. After that, Tom said he made his excuses and fled, much to the relief, I am sure, of Mrs Walsingham. He was gutted not to have had a swim, but maybe it was for the best. Tom and his antics became part of the firm's folklore. The story is probably still being told. Because of his other commitments, Mr Walsingham was often away from the office, and occasionally, Tom would have to see one of his matrimonial clients. He hated this. Sometimes, if the client was a woman, she would get emotional and cry. When this happened, Tom would make an excuse and bolt from his office. He would burst into our room, looking thoroughly panicked and a little wild about the eyes. We would give him a quick pep talk, tell him to man up, arm him with a box of tissues and push him back in. It wasn't only the women who cried. When the men realised how much maintenance they were going to have to pay, some of them shed a few tears.

Sometimes, in the morning when I was waiting for the bus, Tom would come along and give me a lift. It hadn't escaped my notice that not only did he have the same name as the man who took my virginity, but also drove the same make and colour car, a metallic blue Ford Capri but with a black top. I thought it was a sign. Maybe it's the association with the men, but I loved the shape and look of the Capri. They've got one at the car museum in Beaulieu, and I still think it looks good today. Like the Mini, it was a great design. Many years later, it dawned on me that Tom would have had to go out of his way to pass me at the bus stop, but it didn't occur to me then. Dawn was always teasing me and saying, "He likes you. I know he does." Margery was starting to give me dirty looks and had upped the mention of her daughter, but I wasn't sure. I thought he might just like me as a friend. And he was seeing Janice. What I did know for sure was that nothing could ever happen between us whilst I was still married.

I was going to have to tell Danny that I was leaving him.

Chapter 9
More than Words

I ordered a van for my belongings. I was going to have to go back to mother's. My brother James had taken over my bedroom when I had moved out so I would have to have the little 'through room' next to Annie's bedroom. It meant Annie had to walk through my room to get to hers, but beggars can't be choosers. Now I had the unenviable task of breaking the news to Danny. I told him the night before I was due to leave. It did cross my mind just for a minute to leave him a note and just go, but I knew that would be an awful shock when he came in from work, and it would make him as mad as a hell so I braced myself to make the speech of a lifetime.

I sat him down, and I told him I was leaving. I told him he could beat me, he could smash the house up, he could do absolutely anything to me, but he wouldn't stop me. I was going. He asked if I was seeing someone else, and I said I wasn't, which strictly speaking was true. He took it surprisingly calmly. I did lie however when he asked if there was a chance that after a break, I might return. I told him yes, maybe that would happen. I know it was wrong, but I didn't want him to lose his temper. I was very scared of what he might do; he had threatened me so many times. I knew absolutely and with total certainty that I would never go back to him. Not if I was on my own for the rest of my days. But I didn't tell him that. The next day, he went to work early as usual. I didn't see him. The man and van arrived, and we loaded up my few belongings. I only took items I had owned before I moved in with him. A large pine chest of drawers which had stood on the landing of my childhood home in Lee-on-the-Solent. A couple of chairs, some china pots, my little enamel steamer which I bought in the kitchen shop at Habitat, a mirror, my albums, my clothes and my bicycle. Everything else

I left, including all our wedding photos. I wasn't sad in the slightest about leaving the house. I didn't look back.

I was however heartbroken to leave our three cats, Doobie (after the Doobie Brothers), Moonie (after Keith Moon) and Rickenbacker (after the WWI American fighter 'Ace'); I'm joking. There was an American pilot called Rickenbacker, but our cat was named after a character in the Levi jeans advert. We always called him Ricky, and he was Danny's favourite. Leaving the cats was one of the hardest things I have ever had to do. I knew that I had to put my own safety and happiness over theirs, but it was really hard. Mother and her husband now had a little West Highland terrier, so I couldn't take them there. Danny actually liked the cats. It was his job to feed them each morning, and he had bonded with them. He promised me faithfully that he would look after them. That was another reason why I didn't want to make him unnecessarily angry and felt I had to give him some hope that I might return. It was inevitable that I would leave Danny; the marriage was over for me, but I would be lying if I said that Tom wasn't the catalyst. And now the moment had arrived. I was off. If it weren't for the cats, I would have been letting off fireworks, but as the van pulled away, I had mixed feelings. I soon settled back in at home. It was fun being in the next room to Annie. We played music, and we shared clothes and makeup. I felt carefree again. My family never really knew what I had been through with Danny, and they remained very fond of him. They certainly didn't know about all the drug taking. Annie knew how much I liked Tom, but we didn't really discuss it. I think she felt loyal to Danny. My sister Sarah had now got divorced. She had met another croupier in the Bahamas, and they were making plans to return to Britain. My brother had met the girl he was eventually to marry.

Mother's marriage to the creature from the black lagoon was on the rocks. I think the initial appeal was that he was so different than my stepfather. Trog was a party animal and loved nothing better than grabbing the microphone and singing to an audience, usually something by Frank Ifield or Perry Como. I don't think it was around back then, but he would have loved karaoke. My stepfather, on the other hand, was very quiet, and they rarely went out. However, now the scales had well and truly fallen from mother's eyes. The atmosphere in the house was horrible. They literally didn't speak to each other for weeks, maybe even months. He cooked his own meals (well fried them) banging about in the kitchen just to make his point, and he took his washing to the launderette down the road. He was such a git. He even ignored their little dog. She used to rush down to the back gate when he got home, tail wagging nineteen to the dozen, squirming around the way dogs do when they greet you, and he would walk briskly by her with his nose in the air. Didn't even give her a pat. Finally, he packed up his cheap suits and string vests and left. Although mother was relieved to see him go, she was very hurt over yet another failed marriage, and it took her quite a while to bounce back. Also, when her other marriages hit the skids, she was always sure of the next man. Now she was in her fifties and alone. Happily, she still had the dog.

My Lupus was reasonably well controlled. I still had bad evenings, but I think my health had improved now I was no longer in a caustic relationship. Since I was first diagnosed, I had been taking a small dose of steroids each day, and now I was trying out a drug called Hydroxychloroquine, an anti-rheumatic which strangely is also used to treat malaria. I had been to see my GP because I had a lump in my groin. He quickly put my mind at rest. It was a gland (I didn't know you had glands there) and was no doubt stress related, which made perfect sense. My feelings for Tom were all consuming. I played *All in All* (*This One Last Wild Waltz*) by Dexy's Midnight Runners constantly. I must have driven the rest of the house mad. In the end, the whole family were humming it—even my mother. To me, it was Tom's Theme and always will be. My other favourite was *Talk of the Town* by the Pretenders. He still stopped to give me a lift if he saw me at the bus stop, but apart from that, I was no further forward, and he was still with Janice. Then, he invited Dawn and me to a party at his house.

I can't tell you how excited I was. It was an opportunity for him to see me dressed up for once, with makeup. At work, I wore a skirt and top, or trousers, and I very rarely bothered with makeup. I usually overslept in the mornings, so there was never time. Of course when you are in your twenties, you can get away with it. Now if I appeared at work without makeup, I would scare them all to death. Someone would probably throw a blanket over me, or call for a medic. I borrowed a dress from Annie. It was dark fuchsia pink silk with shoestring straps. It clung to my body like a second skin. My hair was shoulder length, light brown with a lot of blond highlights. I wore my usual heavy dark eyeshadow and for once, a pair of stiletto heels. I looked lovely, and I felt lovely as I set off in the taxi.

Tom lived in a small, semi-detached house in Titchfield. He wasn't even thirty, but it was the third house he had owned. It was modern and sparsely furnished. Typical bachelor pad, no ornaments or pictures, very functional. What furniture there was had been pushed to the walls to create floor space. Tom shared the house with his lodger Keith, who was also one of his best friends. If he thought I looked nice; he didn't say, although, I did fancy, I caught him checking me out a couple of times. I finally came face to face with Janice. She was older than me and much taller. Without shoes I was only 5'1" so it wasn't hard. I couldn't say she was ugly, but to me, she seemed a little plain. She had dark hair, although not as dark as Tom's, parted in the middle. It didn't look like she was wearing makeup. It was absolute torture seeing them together. They looked very much an item; she kept touching his arm and never left his side. At one point, I saw them kiss. I was conscious of the fact that she was a solicitor and so must be clever, and she played squash with him, so she was athletic which would have appealed to Tom enormously. My inferiority complex kicked in. All of a sudden, I felt overdressed and over made up. My shoes began to hurt. Luckily, I had Dawn and her boyfriend to talk to, but I just wanted to go home and lick my wounds. It was hard to keep a smile on my face.

Back in the office, things went on much the same between us. The three of us still had a crossword race each lunchtime. I still won. My crush on Tom grew, but I was beginning to lose hope. Flowers from Danny arrived with depressing regularity. I know I sound like a bitch, but they were horrible flowers. You would think that after five years together he would have known I wasn't keen on chrysanthemums, and I hated the colour peach. What did he send? Bouquet after bouquet of peach chrysanthemums. He also phoned a lot to tell me how well he was doing, not drinking, not taking drugs and looking after the cats. I made the mistake of agreeing to go round for tea with him on Sunday. I really didn't want to. I knew it was a mistake, but he wore me down, and I felt sorry for him. I didn't want to hurt him. I wanted him to move on. That Sunday, I cycled round with a heavy heart. He was ridiculously pleased to see me. He tried to hug me, but I was stiff and unyielding. He had laid on a proper tea. Little cakes, tiny sandwiches, little pots of chocolate mousse; it was like a children's tea party. He was on his best behaviour, but he seemed pathetic somehow. I wondered, not for the first time, what I had ever seen in him. The cats looked healthy and happy. When I left, although I told him I would visit again soon, I knew in my heart that I would never set foot in that house again.

Mr Walsingham retired, and a new matrimonial solicitor called Nick joined us. He was fortyish, divorced, incredibly posh and wealthy but enormous fun. Tom and him were like a comedy double act; the office was a fun place to be. One of his first clients was my mother. He got her a good settlement; she kept the house which was only fair as it had been bought with the money from her divorce from my stepfather. Other good news was that Tom and Janice were no longer seeing each other. At first, I was elated, but nothing between us changed and I soon started to worry about all the other women he might meet. I hated it when he had attractive clients, especially if they were single. To add to my woes, he was going on holiday to Portugal for two weeks with a friend. On the one hand, I was going to miss him terribly, but on the other, I was looking forward to having a break from my roller-coaster emotions. At the start of his first week away, when I came into work, I saw he had left me a note. It was basically a step by step guide to all the transactions that were nearing exchange of contracts or completion. What searches to do, when to send the report on title to the Building Society, when to get the clients in to sign. It was an extensive list, all in his neat handwriting now so familiar to me.

And there at the bottom of the page just under his signature, he had put a kiss!

Chapter 10
Perfect Day

I was delirious with happiness. Tom had left me a kiss. I couldn't wait for him to get back. When he did return, he was lovely and brown and full of stories about Portugal. He bought me some perfume, Rive Gauche by Yves Saint Laurent and 200 cigarettes for Dawn. I was so touched. From that moment, I knew that I might really have a chance. With barely contained excitement, I waited for him to make his move. It was to be a long wait. More crosswords, more awkward filing in his office. Once again, my hope was fading. Dawn suggested that I bite the bullet and ask him out, but I couldn't. I was far too scared I might have read it all wrong and he would turn me down. Then one day, I was alone at my desk when he suddenly appeared. I suspect Dawn might have given him a bit of a nudge. He hesitated for a moment and then blurted out, "I must take you out some time," and before I could answer, he shot back to his room and slammed the door. And that was it. Had he asked me out? I didn't know. If he had, then when? After a couple of days and with a lot of encouragement from Dawn, I gathered all my courage, went into his room and said, "Do you want to go for a drink at the weekend?"

He picked me up on Saturday night. I can still remember what I wore. A plain cream Laura Ashley blouse which fastened at the back with mother-of-pearl buttons. It had a small collar and short puffed sleeves. I had on tight jeans made of soft velvet in a lovely dark wine colour. I wore gold hoop earrings and four thin gold bangles which jangled whenever I moved my arm. Tom wore jeans and a white t-shirt. We went to a pub called The Chairmakers. When we got out of the car, he took my hand as we walked into the pub. His hands were soft, but dry like warm silk, just how I'd known they would be. It was a fabulous evening;

the conversation flowed. There were no awkward silences. The alcohol probably helped. I was sorry when the barman called last orders. On the way home, he took me to see where he played hockey each weekend. I was a little shocked when he said he played hockey. I thought it was a girl's game, but of course I now know differently. We parked behind the clubhouse and kissed. I was in heaven. We soon steamed up the car windows. When I thought about it later, I don't think he took his seatbelt off.

The following weekend, we went to London Zoo or ZSL as it is now known. The weather was gorgeous; we were so lucky. We had a brilliant time. I have to say that he wasn't in the least bit romantic. Although he did hold my hand for a while, it was more because he didn't want to lose me in the crowd. He did touch me constantly but only to give me little prods and pinches, rather like an annoying kid brother. I suspect that given half a chance, he might have liked to give me a Chinese burn. We each had an ice lolly. I think his was supposed to be blueberry flavour. Whatever it was, it stained his mouth. For a good hour, his teeth and tongue were bright blue. It wasn't a good look. I was very glad I had opted for lemon. On the way back, we stopped at a pub for a meal and then home. We didn't see a movie, but it was a perfect day.

On our next date, we went back to his house. Keith was there, ironing his judo suit, which he informed me was called a Judogi. He must have been very good as I noticed the belt was black. He seemed really nice; I knew we would be friends. It's always a good thing when your boyfriend's mates approve. Keith had obviously been told to make himself scarce, so he didn't hang around. Tom and I sat on the sofa, and within minutes, we were kissing. I was desperate to get him into bed, but I quickly realised he wasn't going to suggest going upstairs any time soon. I couldn't play the virgin when I had been married for five years. That train had well and truly left the station. So I took the initiative and said, "Let's go to bed." I'm not sure what he had planned for the evening, but I'm pretty sure it wasn't seduction. The bed was rumpled and clearly hadn't been changed. But it was fine; the sheets smelled of the Chanel aftershave he always wore, and I wasn't complaining. Frankly, as our clothes flew in all directions, the sheets were the last thing on my mind. He was still nicely tanned from his recent holiday, apart from the bits that hadn't seen the sun which were very pale. He had just the right amount of dark hair on his chest. Not chimpanzee hairy, but enough to run your fingers through. Thankfully, he didn't have a hairy back. He was covered in moles. You could have played join the dots if you were bored. However, at that moment, boredom was not what I was feeling. Finally, the moment I had been dreaming about for months arrived, and as he pushed himself inside me; I thought I would explode. He was incredibly gentle, and I got the impression, very nervous. Although the sex wasn't wild, it was very good. He certainly didn't embarrass himself. Good sex is as much about your feelings for someone as bedroom gymnastics, and I liked this beautiful, gentle man very much indeed. I stayed the night, spooned against him, and in the morning, we did it all over again.

I was so happy. Back in the office, I had a constant smile on my face. It was hard for me to concentrate. I would have loved to have locked his door and ravished him on his desk, but as his door didn't lock, sadly that would remain a fantasy. We had confessed to Dawn that we had been seeing each other, and she was delighted. Margery however was pissed. Tom continued to churn out his usual huge amount of work. He would dictate onto audio tape, which I would then type. I wore a little set of plastic headphones. Just hearing his voice in my ear made me weak in the knees and damp in the knickers. I had it bad. That week, I started divorce proceedings against Danny. I knew that within a day, he would get the letter outlining my intentions and suggesting he take his own legal advice. I didn't know how he would react. But I soon would. He rang me at work. He said if I didn't stop the divorce and come back, he would have the cats put to sleep. I didn't go back. I was terribly upset about the cats, and as the deadline approached, it got worse, but I knew there was nothing I could do. Tom didn't like cats and was in the process of moving, and anyway I wasn't going to pressurise him into taking them on. Danny was as good as his word. That week, Doobie and Moonie were both put down. Ricky was given a reprieve, either because Danny liked him best or he wanted something in reserve with which to threaten me. Soon after, he found out about me and Tom. Maybe somebody told him or maybe he just put two and two together. He rang to tell me to watch my back. Then he rang Tom and told him to watch his back and that his card was marked. We were both frightened. Tom brazened it out, but I knew he was worried. He started checking his tyres and peering underneath his car before getting in. And we watched each other's backs.

I still had an enlarged gland in my groin. The GP was adamant it was stress. He did ask if I had cut myself on the leg or foot, but I hadn't. I had seen him three times about it; the lump was the size of an egg. I was also back and forth with really itchy underarms. It was driving me crazy. I wanted to scratch all the time. The doctor said it was more than likely an allergy. He suggested I stop using deodorant for a while (just what you want to hear at the height of summer) and change my washing powder. I felt he thought I was fussing over nothing, and I probably was.

Tom moved. His lodger Keith had also bought a place of his own and so wasn't going with him. On a lovely summer's evening after work, Tom took me to see his new house. Swanmore was a little village about fourteen miles from Gosport. It felt further; it seemed like we had been driving for ages. It was right out in the country, down long winding unlit roads; the trees sometimes forming green tunnels with their branches. We passed a handful of quaint chocolate box country pubs. Tom's house was in the heart of the village which comprised a pub, a small general store, a butchers and a delicatessen. Just along the road was a primary school which reminded me very much of my first school in Isfield. There was also a picturesque old church built of grey Flintstone. The surrounding graveyard was slightly overgrown, but the many varieties of grasses interwoven with long-stemmed daisies, cornflowers, poppies and stately foxgloves added to the beauty. Some of the gravestones looked ancient, covered in lichen and leaning precariously. The access road to Tom's house was a narrow, muddy lane full of potholes and the car bounced around as we made our approach. The house stood at the far end of a small cul-de-sac in which there were four other houses. It was a newish house, about five years old, built of red brick. It had a drive and a garage. It looked very smart, so far removed from our shabby little terrace on the main road in Gosport. Downstairs there was a large hall with cloakroom off a big lounge/dining room with a beautiful feature fireplace and a kitchen, which was small. Upstairs were three bedrooms and a large bathroom. Patio doors opened from the lounge to the rear garden which was completely enclosed by a high red brick wall. "I'm glad you like it," said Tom. "I was hoping that once your divorce was through, you would come and live with me."

And so our romance gathered in intensity. I met most of his friends. In the main, they were either solicitors, estate agents or insurance brokers. One of the girls was a reporter for *The Evening News* which had a huge circulation back then. Several of the men played hockey with Tom. They were so different from Danny's friends. Not necessarily nicer, just different. Tom and his friends all called each other either by their surnames, or their nicknames. I think it was a public school thing. I didn't much want to meet 'Shitty Mick'. It goes without saying that none of them took drugs. No one even smoked; I was the only smoker. Whenever we went to anyone's house, they would rush to get me a saucer or a little foil tray for my cigarette ash, assuming they didn't own an ashtray of course. I feel bad now that I never went outside to smoke. Just one cigarette can stink your house out for days, and I practically chain smoked back then. They must have been airing out their houses for weeks after I left. At the weekend, someone usually had a dinner party or a barbecue. One chap who owned his own estate agency had a huge property out in the sticks, and he had a barn dance every summer. We grabbed our partners and dosey doed late into the night; it was great fun. We went out either in couples, or as a group to country pubs and nice restaurants. Danny and I never ate out. We did get takeaways occasionally, and I think we went to a Harvesters once. He was banned from most of the Indian and Chinese restaurants around Gosport and Fareham either for fighting or 'doing a runner' i.e. making off without paying. With Tom, a whole new world was opening up before me. Tom's friends all had tales to tell about him. When they were eighteen, a group of them had gone to the South of France. They headed straight for a well-known nudist beach, and all stripped off get an all-over tan. Keith said Tom spent the entire day hunched over with a book strategically placed over his privates. He swore that at the end of the day Tom had a white patch in the exact shape of a paperback. All the lads hooked up with girls at some stage apart from Tom who happily sat at the bar drinking his beer and watching football on the overhead TV. They also told me that I was his first steady girlfriend. Loads of women fancied him, and he had quite a few one-nighters, but he never took things further. Only a couple of his mates had ever met Janice. Tom was also ribbed ceaselessly over the fact that at work he was either impossible to get hold of or if you did get through he would say, "I'll ring you back," and never did. They always had to chase him. Sometimes this would go on for days. One friend said that for a long time he was convinced that Tom didn't actually exist as he never once managed to speak to him.

I hadn't yet met his parents. They lived nearby in Lee-on-the Solent where I had grown up. I was happy that he seemed to be in no hurry to introduce me; it was a meeting I was rather dreading. A couple of his friends asked if I had met his mother and exchanged knowing glances. Apparently, she absolutely doted on Tom. Every Sunday come rain or shine, she would stand on the side lines, clutching a Thermos flask of hot coffee and cheer him on at hockey. She never missed. She never bothered to go and watch his younger sister at the countless gymkhanas she took part in. It was obvious that Tom was the golden boy.

Usually on Sundays, Tom would pick me up after hockey, and we would drive out somewhere for lunch. He was always, always late. Sometimes by well over an hour. It drove me absolutely mad. There is nothing worse than being all ready to go and waiting for someone. I don't know why I bothered getting ready for the arranged time, I always ended up waiting. My family would start to look decidedly nervous, wondering how they would deal with me if he were a no show. Mother had the brandy on standby. Of course, I should have taken into account the fact that post match, they all had to shower and meet in the club bar to rehash the highs and lows of the game, but then he should have allowed for it. Instead, he always said he would pick me up at a time he knew very well he was never going to make. Once he did arrive, and we were on our way; my bad mood quickly evaporated. It was impossible to stay cross with him.

We did have one day out that was memorable for all the wrong reasons. I had been lucky enough to get tickets to see David Bowie at Milton Keynes. It was an open air concert. I prefer indoor concerts; the acoustics are better, and it's a whole lot easier to get to the loo—and nicer when you get there. Outdoor events nearly always have portaloos, and the flushes never work for long. However, I was thrilled to be seeing Bowie again and persuaded Tom to come with me. It would turn out to be a big mistake. We drove to Milton Keynes. It was a really hot day, and as soon as we arrived, we were caught in the slow moving queue of traffic heading for the venue. We crawled along for a couple of miles, the tailback was ridiculous, and with all the stopping and starting, Tom's car kept overheating. He was in a seriously bad mood, made worse because we were hungry and thirsty. He could be sulky and petulant when in a mood. It was a horrible journey; we hardly exchanged two words. I thought Bowie was wonderful, but Tom looked out of place and uncomfortable. I think by that time he had made up his mind not to enjoy himself. It's never the same when you don't know any of the songs. I knew Tom didn't like Bowie's music. I should have gone with a friend. I thought it would be a wonderful shared experience, but I couldn't have been more wrong. It was all a bit of a disaster.

Back home, Annie told me that she had heard that Danny had been stabbed and that it was serious. She worked as a barmaid in a pub which Danny and his friends frequented and someone there had told her. He was in hospital in a critical condition, and he was asking for his wife. My divorce from Danny had reached the decree nisi stage. I just had to apply for the decree absolute, and it would be over. It may seem hard, but I wasn't even tempted to go to the hospital. I knew he would just try to emotionally blackmail me into halting the divorce, or worse to go back to him; neither of which I was going to do. He had put me through hell, and I couldn't forgive and forget. Annie went to see him and so did my mother. They said he looked really pitiful. He had been stabbed with a serrated knife, possibly a bread knife, in the stomach. It had been touch and go. Annie said there was a clear plastic dome, like an upturned bowl on his belly, and underneath his internal organs were completely exposed. Danny told her that he had been jumped in an alley and stabbed for no reason. It later transpired that the man who stabbed him was a teenager who Danny had been threatening for some time. It was Danny who had chased the young man into the alley and cornered him. The youth had stabbed Danny in self-defence.

Danny was in hospital for a couple of months. When he came out, Annie went to see him. She told me he had lost an awful lot of muscle and looked thin and frail. He had a colostomy bag which he would proudly show to all and sundry. He was especially pleased whenever he got gas because it inflated. But it was going to be a long road to recovery for him. For protection, he had bought a German Shepherd puppy.

Chapter 11
Friday on My Mind

Words can't really describe how happy I was when my decree absolute arrived in the post. I was tempted to frame it. I was with a wonderful man, and I could forget those five wasted years with Danny. My sister had also had found happiness with her new man, Martin, and they had married in Nassau. Now they were back in Britain having bought a flat in Wimbledon. They were both working in a London casino. Once again a small van was hired, and my few belongings transported to Tom's house in the country. Tom was such a darling. He knew how worried I was about my cat in Gosport. Now that Danny had a dog, I suspected he would quickly lose interest in Ricky. Also, the house was being repossessed as the mortgage was so far in arrears. Even though he didn't much like cats, Tom told me to go and get Ricky. We would give him a home. Next day, I crept along the alley at the back of my old house, carrying a sturdy cardboard box. It couldn't have gone better. Almost immediately I spotted Ricky in the back garden, and he trotted up to see me. As I picked him up, I could feel how rough and matted his fur was. He was full of scabs and his collar was filthy. He looked as though he had been living outside, possibly to avoid the dog. He wasn't thin so he had been fed. I posted a note through the letterbox to say I had taken him, but I never heard a word from Danny. He was probably relieved. Ricky settled in brilliantly with us. His fur was soon soft and shiny again. He had a lovely nature, and Tom fell in love with him. It wasn't long before he suggested getting a kitten. We looked through a couple of books and decided we would really like a Burmese. Our local vet put us in touch with a breeder in Bournemouth, and soon we had a new addition to our family, a twelve week old lilac Burmese kitten who we called Oliver and who immediately stole our hearts. Tom became a cat lover practically overnight. He would potter in the kitchen, Ricky winding round his feet, and Oliver lying stretched across the back of his neck like a fur stole.

Life was good. I finally met his parents. They had a nice property in Lee-on-the Solent, crammed with antiques and beautiful furniture. Everything was old but quality. The living room smelled of beeswax furniture polish. Tom's mother was called Jane. Like Tom, she was very tall. She stood ramrod straight, and although she was well into her seventies, was fit and vital. Her hair was neatly fashioned in the style I call 'the cauliflower head' – beloved of mature ladies the world over. I learnt later that she had her hair set each week, unlike my mother who only visited the hairdresser on high days and holidays and had been known to cut her own. She wore glasses. Like Tom, she was reserved and difficult to talk to. She put me in mind of a Victorian matriarch. Not the sort of person you would want to get stuck in a broken down lift with. 'Buttoned up' would best describe her. I'm sure I must have come as a bit of a shock. I couldn't have been the type of girl she would have wanted for her son. I was newly divorced, I smoked, and I had a chronic illness. Thank goodness she didn't know about the drugs. Whatever her true feelings, she was far too well bred to let it show, and she did her best to make me welcome.

Tom's father was called Godfrey. He was much shorter than Tom and his mother and was bald with glasses. The minute I saw him, I was amazed at his uncanny resemblance to John Reginald Halliday Christie of 10 Rillington Place fame. Godfrey however was a sweetheart. I couldn't see him strangling someone and stuffing them under the floorboards. Although, the way Jane bitched at him, it may well have crossed his mind. He was never without a cigarette and never without a glass of whiskey. I loved him. He was my kind of guy. The marriage had not been happy. They had stayed together very much for the children and also because divorce was frowned on in their day, unless you were my mother of course. Tom and his two sisters very much sided with their mother, and Tom's relationship with his father was strained at best. Tom's father had also been a solicitor but retirement had left him with a void in his life; a void he filled with drink. He was usually pissed by mid-morning. As a young man, he had played rugby and sailed. I believe he and a friend did an Atlantic crossing in their small yacht. But these weren't activities that could be carried on into old age. In all the time I knew him, he never, ever got my name right. He would call me anything so long as it began with the letter 'E'; 'Eileen' was a particular favourite, but he rang the changes with 'Elsie'. It didn't matter how many times we all shouted, "It's Ellie," he never got it. He also repeated himself all the time. He would ask you a question, then five minutes later, he would ask the same thing again. Whether this was the drink, senility or he was just bored with us and wasn't really listening, we never knew, but in all probability, it was the drink. He also coughed a lot, and it was rather phlegmy and disgusting.

The whole family were 'foodies'. Jane was a fabulous cook. Everything was home made. Every Sunday they would have a large joint and Jane would make stuffing with fresh breadcrumbs and onion and sage picked from the garden. You wouldn't have found any Paxo in her cupboard. The same went for the mint sauce to go with lamb; it was properly made with fresh mint. She even made horse-radish sauce from horse-radish grown in the garden. Tom and his father loved things like Gentleman's Relish and Arbroath Smokies or devilled kidneys for breakfast. Jane pressed her own ox-tongue and would boil up a whole pig's head to make brawn. Gramps would have loved her. If Godfrey could get his meat 'on the hoof', he did. Most weekends, something would be plucked, skinned and gutted for the table. Tom told me that at Christmas their turkey would be specially ordered to still have its head and feathers. Jane would spend an entire morning happily plucking away. I suppose it's a small mercy the turkey was dead. Godfrey absolutely refused to eat anything Italian. This was because of the War. Rice was also vetoed because the Japanese couldn't be trusted or forgiven. Rice pudding was however allowed. Obviously nothing German would be tolerated in any way shape or form. Most Sundays, we would go to Tom's parents for dinner. Keith always joined us; it was a tradition. We all sat round the large oak table with its ball and claw feet. There was a starched tablecloth and proper napkins in silver napkin rings on which each member of the family had their initials engraved. At my mother's house, we had a tray on our laps in front of the TV. Obviously, there was no tablecloth because we didn't have a table and a sheet of kitchen roll served for a napkin.

Godfrey would always carve the joint. First, he would sharpen the knife using a long honing steel. I hate the sound of knives being sharpened, and Godfrey went on for ages; I would have to discretely put my fingers in my ears to block out the noise. Then he would have a coughing fit over the meat. Jane would give him a frosty look, but he took absolutely no notice. I honestly think he did it on purpose just to annoy her. Finally, he would start to carve. He used a large two pronged fork to spear the meat, and as we eagerly held out our plates, he would shake the meat laden fork over each plate in turn. The thing is, no meat ever fell off. He didn't seem to notice; by then, he had moved on to the next person and was shaking the fork over their plate. When he had gone round everyone and put down the carving implements, our plates were still completely bare. Someone would have to deploy a distraction using the roast potatoes or gravy whilst the rest of us would dive onto the joint to grab what meat we could. If by some rare and happy chance, something did drop from Godfrey's carving fork, you could be sure it would be all fat. I always said, "Could I have a lean bit please, Godfrey," and he would say, "A lean bit for Eileen coming right up," and deposit a mass of wobbling yellow fat and grey gristle on my plate. By the time we did eventually start eating, it was all cold. Keith and I frequently got the giggles; we were like two naughty kids. No one else was amused. I dreaded it if the beef was on the menu. I like my beef to be pink, but theirs was literally raw. A decent vet could have got it back on its feet. It was horrible. My heart also sank if we had pheasant. Godfrey liked his pheasant to be really ripe and smelly; I think the term is 'high'. You were just about getting to it before the maggots. Also, it was always riddled with shot which could play havoc with your fillings. We all made neat little heaps on the edge of our plates, like a stockpile of cannonballs in miniature. Thankfully, there was always plenty of wine with the meal and port or liqueurs after. We never had wine growing up. We never had drink in the house at all except at Christmas. Tom's parents had a massive stock of booze. Pretty much anything you could think of; it was like being in a pub only without the cheerful atmosphere.

I was crazy in love with Tom, but I was disappointed with our sex life. I knew he didn't have a lot of experience, but I had thought that once he got a taste for it, he would turn into a tiger in the bedroom. It wasn't happening. We did make love but not nearly so often as I would have liked. Hell, I would have liked it twice a day. I could barely keep my hands off him. I know the experts would say you have to communicate, tell your partner what you want. But I couldn't do it. Believe it or not, I could be quite shy, and I had always relied on the man to take the lead. I was in a whole new territory. I tried everything. I would call him in to wash my back when I was in the bath. He would grab the sponge and sluice me down like he was washing the car. When he had finished, he would wring the sponge out over my hair. Hair that I had taken some considerable time pinning and arranging seductively. Or he would splosh the wet sponge into my face before disappearing back downstairs. On one occasion, I put on a little black and red lace corset together with black stockings and suspenders. I sat in front of the mirror drying my hair, taking my time and deliberately posing. He was on the bed reading a cookery book. I could see him staring at me intently, and I thought *Oy, Oy—it's working*. Then he said, "That hairdryer's bloody noisy isn't it?" and went back to his book. I tried pressing myself up against him in bed, I threw my leg across him. I was like a dog on heat, but it had no effect. I tried to edge his hand down in the right direction, but as soon as he was about to achieve touchdown, he whipped his hand away like he had encountered something hot, which quite frankly, he very nearly had. Once I tried giving him little feathery kisses, starting on his scrummy chest and moving slowly south. I got to just under his belly button when he practically yanked me back by my hair. What man turns down a BJ? Not one I had ever met that's for sure. I was baffled. I finally decided that maybe I was coming on too strong and scaring him so I tried to be patient. It wasn't easy. I was beginning to realise how Danny must have felt. I didn't doubt for a second that Tom loved me. He was incredibly affectionate, always touching me and following me around. When he looked at me, I could see the love light in his eyes. He spoilt me rotten. I had enough perfume to stock a small shop. Chanel, Dior, Estee Lauder. My skin cream was by Clinique and Lancôme. We ate in lovely pubs and restaurants; I really couldn't complain. One day when I got home, there were two brand new cars in the drive. A blue Peugeot 205 for me and a white 205 GTI for him. Because they had come off the production line together, we had consecutive number plates, which was rather cool.

As Sarah and her new husband Martin were now settled in their Wimbledon flat, I was visiting them for the week. Tom had too much on in the office. He was going to drive up on Friday after work, and we would have the weekend together. I travelled up by train the Saturday before. Sarah looked fit and well; she was still tanned from her time in Nassau. Her husband Martin was extremely pale with almost black hair and a drooping moustache. His colouring was very similar to Tom's, but he didn't look anywhere near as healthy. He was very slim, a little weedy if I'm honest. He gave the impression of someone who had never seen daylight. He made me think of a vampire, although, he wasn't unattractive. He was very sweet but extremely quiet. In comparison, Tom seemed positively loud. Privately, I wondered how long he would hold my sister's interest. I thought him nice but dull. The flat was amazing. It was situated in a leafy road in the heart of Wimbledon. It was all polished wooden floors and recessed lighting. The enormous front room had a floor to ceiling bay window, and there was a fabulous three-piece suite with off-white linen covers and large squashy cushions. The whole flat was on three levels; it was very impressive. Tom and I would be sleeping in the smaller of the two bedrooms, but for now, of course, I was on my own. Sarah and Martin were both working at Maxims, an exclusive casino in Kensington. Sarah was an inspector there and had swapped her bunny costume for a glamourous black evening dress. Martin dealt blackjack or sometimes worked the craps table, a game in which punters bet on the roll of a pair of dice. Between them, they were earning really good money. We had a brilliant week sight-seeing in London. We went to see Joni Mitchell at the Theatre Royal Drury Lane. I didn't really know her music, only *Big Yellow Taxi* and *Both Sides Now*, but I thoroughly enjoyed the concert. At night, Martin and Sarah were working so I had the flat to myself. I was love sick. I couldn't wait to see Tom. I had butterflies in my tummy just thinking about him. I remember listening to *Every Breath You Take* by the Police over and over and yearning for him.

Eventually, Friday evening arrived and with it, my lovely man. He looked so handsome. Away from the office, he always wore jeans usually with a Pringle V-neck jumper, or a t-shirt if the weather was warm. He was tall, dark and handsome, and I loved him. He was so happy to see me and gave me a long hug. Introductions made, we went to a ranch-style steak house for dinner and feasted on spicy chicken wings, barbecue ribs and loaded potato skins. I don't think Sarah liked Tom awfully. Like his mother, Tom could be quite difficult to chat to. If he was in the mood, no one was better company. He could be witty and engaging and bright. If he wasn't in the mood, talking to him was like pulling teeth; he could be hard work and could seem disinterested and bored. I found it so frustrating. I wanted people to love him like I did. I could see Sarah had her reservations. That night we made love, but it was a real quickie and not the reunion I had been anticipating all week. Still, he had been at work all day and then driven up to London; I was being unreasonable to expect too much. Over the weekend, we did all the usual touristy things. On Saturday evening, we went to Michel Roux Jnr's Le Gavroche. As you would expect, the food was to die for. I think Tom would have liked larger portions, but boy, it tasted good. On Sunday afternoon. we went to The Hard Rock Cafe in Old Park Lane. That was my favourite. The hot fudge sundae was pure heaven. Then we said our goodbyes and headed home. It was nice to be on our own again.

Our first Christmas together was everything I could have dreamt of. We had a real tree and it looked beautiful. We had a job keeping Oliver away. He kept knocking the baubles off the tree and trying to climb up it. We were concerned he might electrocute himself. He was also fond of running up the curtains. He would go right to the top and hang there looking down on us, but we couldn't be cross. On Christmas Eve, we went to a party at Keith's house, but we left quite early to be fresh for Christmas Day. I had bought Tom a dark chocolate brown double length sheepskin rug for the front room, a red cashmere jumper and some of his favourite Chanel aftershave. I had also bought a stuffed lion from Hamleys Toy Shop in London because Tom was a Leo, and I thought he might like it. It had cost me a small fortune. I have to say Tom didn't seem terribly impressed, but he loved everything else. I got Chanel perfume with matching body cream and shower gel, some Diorella perfume and talc, a black angora jumper and a beautiful china Royal Doulton crinoline lady figurine. We went for Christmas dinner at his parents. Keith was there, and so were Tom's sisters. Tom's elder sister Pamela was accompanied by her husband and three children. She was ten years older than Tom. She was incredibly loud. You wouldn't have thought she came from the same family. You could hear her laugh from a mile away, possibly several and her voice was like a foghorn. She was very 'jolly hockey sticks'. She never swore, but used the word 'Bally' in almost every sentence. She also said 'Golly' quite a lot and 'Gosh'. I never actually heard her say 'What Ho' or 'By Jove', but I imagine she did. Her husband was something high up in the Royal Navy. and I got the impression he was more than a little hen-pecked. He must surely have been a little deaf. Tom's younger sister was called Helen. She was a year younger than Tom. She was single and worked as a chef. She was stocky with a large matronly bust. She had short hair and never wore make-up. She suffered greatly with allergies and always sounded nasal. But she was lovely, and we got on very well. She had a definite soft spot for Keith, but as he had known her for so long; he looked on her as more of a sister than a potential girlfriend. So we all put on our paper hats, pulled our crackers and waited patiently for Godfrey to sharpen his carving knife, have a good cough and wave the meat over our plates. The large Christmas pudding doused with brandy burnt spectacularly. After dinner, we played charades. It didn't matter what film or book title Godfrey was given, he did exactly the same mime for each, which mainly involved stomping up and down and windmilling his arms. We would all shout out the names of completely random films and books until he eventually got flustered and sat down in a huff. We stuffed ourselves with nuts and chocolates and homemade mince pies with brandy butter. Later, there was a selection of cheese and biscuits. Then, it was back to Swanmore and our happy home. Tired and over full, we were soon asleep with Ricky and Oliver curled up together at the foot of our bed.

Chapter 12
Spanish Stroll

We were off to Spain. One of the firm's partners had a villa in Nerja on the Costa Del Sol and was letting us have it for two weeks. Apart from school trips to France and Guernsey, I had never been abroad. I didn't count being born in Canada as obviously I couldn't remember that. It was all incredibly exciting. As a child, Tom had often gone with his family to France during school holidays. Occasionally, they went to Portugal, which was Tom's favourite holiday destination. He loved the people and the food. Our family usually went to either Devon or Cornwall where we would stay in a caravan. I have to say, we always had a good time. Nanny took Sarah and me away a few times. We went pony trekking in Somerset which we both loved. Nanny chilled in the hotel whilst we were out riding. Sarah was a fairly accomplished rider and was given a gorgeous spirited pony with a glossy chestnut coat. She would canter off, weaving through the trees, jumping fallen logs and generally having a blast. I was on a small Shetland pony with a huge round belly. He had one speed and that was slow. I honestly think if a bomb had gone off behind him, he wouldn't have increased his pace. He farted constantly, really loudly. Because I couldn't ride very well, I was on a leading rein attached to the riding instructor She was a dragon. My pony was dead greedy; all he wanted to do was munch the vegetation and she would shriek, "Don't let him eat. Keep his head up. Keep his head up." Let me tell you, stopping a horse from lowering its head if that's what it has a mind to do is nigh on impossible. I was pulling on the reins, standing up in the stirrups, and I couldn't do it. I was forever being told off.

Tom and I had something to celebrate. He was being made a partner. That would mean a share in the firm's profits and a company car. The firm already gave Tom an allowance for petrol which was so generous; it pretty much covered my petrol as well. Tom usually did all the driving, so my mileage wasn't high. When we got back from holiday, I would be moving to the firm's office in Fareham to work for the same partner who was lending us the villa. His name was Steven, and he was the firm's senior partner. I loved working with Tom, but as we were now living together, we both thought it better if I were to move. The day before we were due to leave, we boarded the cats. We now had four. We had given a home to a little black male we got from the RSPCA. He was eight months old. He was the most laid back cat I have ever known. You didn't even have to hold him to give him a worming pill. You could just tilt his head back, pop the tablet in the side of his mouth, and he would swallow it. We called him Rasputin, but usually Raz. The other cat was a Devon Rex kitten who we called Sam. It would be the start of my love affair with Devon Rexes. They are just the best cats ever. They stay playful for their whole lives; they are inquisitive and loyal. I just love their little bald necks and teddy bear fur, their huge bat-like ears and stubby whiskers. Also they don't moult.

It was at an ungodly hour on a chilly September morning that we set off on our first holiday together. I thoroughly enjoyed the flight. I sat with my nose pressed to the window and marvelled at the view with the wonder of a child. The neat green patchwork fields, the sea dotted with tiny boats leaving v-shaped wakes on the surface of the water, the craggy grey mountains and the sheer beauty of the clouds. As I was pretty sure joining the Mile High Club wasn't an option, I settled for a large gin and tonic instead. At Malaga airport we collected our hire car. Steven and Julia's villa was about an hour and a half's drive along the coast. It was really hot. I hadn't ever experienced such heat, but I loved it. We stopped at a little cafe at the side of the road and had prawns pil pil with crusty bread. I couldn't believe the size of the rubber trees, and they were everywhere. I was so proud when my rubber plant at home got a new leaf, I didn't know they could grow into actual trees. And of course, there were avocados and apricots, peaches, oranges and lemons; it seemed like paradise. In Britain, if we get a month in summer with no rain (extremely rare I know), there are immediate calls for a hosepipe ban, and we are all told to restrict our water use. In Spain, it's baking hot for months on end; every other house has a swimming pool, and everywhere you look is lush and verdant. Go figure.

The villa was at the top of a steep hill overlooking a holiday complex called El Capistrano. All the buildings were white, typical of Mediterranean villages everywhere. The walls were festooned with jasmine, passion flower and brilliant pink and orange Bougainvillea. Prickly pear cactus grew in large thickets. The maid service had been and left clean sheets and towels. There was a cold bottle of champagne in the fridge. There was a large double bedroom, a lounge, bathroom and kitchen. There was a balcony with a built in barbecue pit. No prizes for guessing what I would have most liked to do at that moment, but that definitely wasn't on the cards. Tom wanted a drink and a swim. I would have to wait.

It was the most magical time. There were three swimming pools within the complex. We liked the smaller of the three. Often, we had the pool to ourselves. There was a bar right next to it called The Cave Bar, which funnily enough was exactly like a cave. We spent a lot of time in there necking cold San Miguel's and eating tapas. I adored the evenings. Wandering round in a strappy top, the air filled with the scent of jasmine mingling with the mouth-watering aroma of chickens cooking on the rotisserie outside the little supermarket. I never tired of seeing the tiny lizards darting about and hearing the sound of thousands of chirping crickets. There were coloured spotlights dotted amongst the plants; it really was like fairyland. All the shops stayed open for most of the night. We treated ourselves to some Lladro as it was so cheap. Some days we went to the beach where I threw caution and my bikini top to the wind. We ate in one of the many beach bars. The seafront wasn't developed; it was all very shanty town but to us that added to the appeal. We both got so brown. I don't think I have ever looked or felt so good. My lupus seemed to vanish; it gave me no trouble at all for the whole fortnight; I wanted to stay forever.

Tom's favourite thing was to drive up into the mountains, off the beaten track to find places where only the locals ate. He would stop at some little out of the way restaurant where it was all very basic. There were always a lot of scrawny chickens grubbing about in the dirt outside. You just knew that if you ordered chicken, the chef would leap out with his cleaver and chase them around. That's probably why they are all so thin, they do so much running. You certainly wouldn't want to be the chicken with the gammy leg. Sometimes the host would grab Tom by the arm and steer him into the kitchen to taste whatever was simmering in his pot. He spoke no English, Tom spoke no Spanish so there was a good deal of face pulling and gesticulation. Privately, I didn't think it was a restaurant, I think it was just somebody's house. Whatever, they seemed very happy to show Tom their kitchen. I had hoped that being on holiday, somewhere warm and exotic would fire Tom up in the bedroom. But despite all my best efforts and womanly wiles, that was not the case. We had the sun, sea and sangria, but the sex, I am sad to say, was in short supply. However, we did manage a few times, and, all in all, it had been a wonderful, wonderful first holiday. Tom had his new partnership to look forward to; it seemed we were living the dream.

Back at home, the cats had survived their ordeal in the cattery and were pleased to see us. I started my job at Fareham Office. Steven had two secretaries, me and Debbie. She was a hoot; we had the same sense of humour. He mostly did criminal work, but also some conveyancing. He was also the Deputy Coroner. Steven was nice but very scary. He could be extremely cutting. I've seen grown men leaving his room in tears. He certainly didn't tolerate fools. He could be really friendly and smile and chat but the next time would totally ignore you—cut you dead. He ran everywhere and always took the stairs two at a time. His wife Julia was great. All the other partners' wives were rather stuffy and full of their own perceived importance. Julia was completely down to earth and somewhat eccentric. She smoked like a chimney (even more than me) and drank black coffee by the gallon. Her lipstick was always smudged above her lip line and over her teeth; she called everyone 'darling' and was fond of brightly-coloured pashminas. She took me under her wing, we were kindred spirits. On my second day at Fareham, Tom came up for a meeting with Steven about his partnership. He brought our two packs of holiday snaps to bore poor Steven with. Everyone wanted a look so the photos went all round the office, about thirty people. Afterwards, I said to Tom, "You did take out the pictures of me topless, didn't you?" Of course he didn't. I wondered why everyone had been so keen to see them. It was days before I could look any of the men in the eye.

I finally got round to registering myself with the local doctor. I had to go in to meet him and discuss my lupus. He was a young man but had a real air of competence about him, I immediately felt I was in safe hands. He read my notes and commented that the gland in my groin had been enlarged for quite some time. He thought I should go to the hospital for a biopsy, which just over a week later, I did. Afterwards, the site from where they had taken the biopsy wouldn't heal. It wasn't infected, it just constantly wept lymph serum. I had to go daily to the nurse to have the cavity packed with a dressing; it was a real nuisance. Days later, I drove myself to Queen Alexandra Hospital to see the consultant for the result of the biopsy. I trotted in, and he said with no preamble, "I'm afraid you've got cancer, and we need to start you on chemotherapy immediately." He went on to say that the cancer I had was called Non Hodgkin's Lymphoma. He told me that if I responded well to the treatment, I had an 80% chance of survival which are pretty good odds. But I barely took it in. I cried all the way home. I could hardly see to drive. I wanted Tom.

Chapter 13
Die Another Day

Tom held me as I cried. I was frightened, it was such a shock. I had felt so well in Spain, and I still didn't feel ill. Never had I once suspected the lump in my groin was cancer. Even when I went for the biopsy, cancer hadn't crossed my mind. I had seen the doctor in Gosport on several occasions, and he was never concerned. I had complained two or three times about itching and the enlarged gland, symptoms which taken together I now knew could be indicative of Non Hodgkin's Lymphoma. Moving to Swanmore to be with Tom had possibly saved my life, although, I knew I had a battle ahead of me.

I started chemotherapy almost immediately. I had Stage 2 Non Hodgkin's Lymphoma which meant I had other tumours. A CT scan confirmed these to be in my chest and neck. Tom's mother took me to my first appointment at St Mary's Hospital in Portsmouth. She ended up taking me to most of my appointments as Tom was always so tied up at work. The clinic was extremely busy. So many people with cancer. All different ages. Some looked really ill, some looked really well. A lot were wearing wigs or had scarves tied around their heads. We had to wait for a long time, but eventually, I was summoned to a small room for my first treatment. The cocktail of drugs was administered through an intravenous catheter or IV in the back of my hand. It felt very cold as the mixture went in. I was to have chemotherapy every two weeks. After the treatment, despite Jane's misgivings, I went back to work. All the while, I was thinking, *Well that was a doddle. I don't know what the fuss is about.* Then suddenly I started to feel ill, and I wanted to lie down. Steven took me home. By then, I was feeling very nauseous. Sweat was pouring off me. My mouth started to water, and I knew I was going to hurl. I was dreadfully sick, I had to catch it in my jumper. I wasn't exactly relaxed around Steven at the best of times, and now I was vomiting in his posh car. He was very kind. He helped me indoors and up to the bedroom. Thankfully, he didn't suggest helping me undress. He had called Tom, who was on his way, and he waited downstairs until Tom arrived. I crawled under the duvet, wallowing in misery and reflecting on the fact that this might not be such a doddle after all.

The next couple of sessions left me equally unwell. I didn't attempt to go back to work, Jane took me straight home. I began to dread having the IV inserted and the strong smell of the chemicals as they ran into the line. Sometimes, because your veins had collapsed, other sites had to be found for the IV. A couple of times, the needle was put in my foot. The chemo left me nauseous and completely zapped of energy. After a few days, I would just begin to perk up, and it would be time for the next session. The one good thing was the comradery and support of the other patients and their relatives. We were all willing each other on. The doctors and nurses were wonderful too; their job can't have been easy. Coincidentally, a chap who worked in our office in Portsmouth was also having treatment for Hodgkin's. His name was Bob. This was his second bout of chemo because the disease had come back after a spell in remission. He was only in his thirties with a young family, and we were all praying that this time the chemotherapy would work. I was told that my hair would eventually fall out, but to slow down the hair loss, I could try scalp hypothermia treatment. This involved sitting for about thirty minutes attached to a machine and wearing a cooling cap. The cold constricts the blood vessels in the scalp which reduces the amount of chemotherapy reaching the hair follicles. It was extremely unpleasant, like having your head put in the freezer for half an hour.

Tom and I tried to carry on with our lives as normally as possible. I was still able to work, although, I usually had the day after my chemotherapy off. Tom was as busy as ever. He was always the firm's top fee earner; no one else even came close. He had the amazing ability to know without having to consult the files exactly what stage each transaction was at. His client's really loved him, and the recommendations poured in. He probably had double the case load of the other conveyancer's in the firm. It always amazed me that his desk was so tidy, nothing out of place, everything lined up neatly. He only ever had one pen, whereas I needed to have at least thirty strewn around, to be sure of finding one when I needed it. He was very hardworking; it was unheard of for him to be off sick. He would be in his office by 7.00am in order to miss the rush hour traffic. It also enabled him to open his mountain of post and get his dictation done before the office officially opened at nine. His new secretary was called Laura, and I was more than a little bit envious of her.

Christmas was soon upon us. On Christmas Eve, Keith came up. We were going to walk round the corner to our local and had arranged to meet some other friends there. It was a great local, always busy with a real wood fire. Tom said the beer was good and the food certainly was. The landlord always gave us a big welcome and would often stand us the first drink. He always called Tom 'Ian', and we never had the heart to correct him. I hadn't yet lost my hair, but it was noticeably thinner. I decided to pin it up. As I was opening a hairgrip with my teeth, one of my top front crowns pinged off, leaving me with a little black stump. I already felt undesirable and unattractive, and this seemed like the last straw. My hair was straggly, and I had a black stump for a front tooth. I looked like a witch; all I was missing was a wart. My immediate reaction was to say I wasn't going out, but Tom and Keith rallied me. Within ten minutes, they were teasing me, singing *All I Want for Christmas is My Two Front Teeth* and saying, "Sorry, did you whistle?" every time I spoke. But it did the trick. Soon I was laughing, albeit with my hand over my mouth. After Christmas, my chemo continued. I had to have a bone marrow test to check that the cancer hadn't spread. Although the test is very quick, it is the most painful procedure you can ever imagine. People went into the room looking a little nervous, but quite composed and came out clutching tissues and openly weeping. When the doctor actually tells you he is sorry, but this is really going to hurt, you know you've got to brace yourself.

My hair was now falling out in clumps. I kept it in a carrier bag, and it wasn't long before the bag was full. I shaved off the final few wispy bits. Being without hair makes you feel so vulnerable and exposed. How you would imagine being naked in public would feel. I had feared losing my hair more than the actual cancer. All my body hair also fell out, pubes, underarms and legs. My eyebrows and eyelashes weren't affected. The NHS supplied two wigs. I chose a short bob and one that can only be described as the Louis XIV look. What was I thinking? As my head is quite small, the sides of the wig covered my ears. At work if I was talking on the phone, which I frequently did, I had to pull the wig up at the sides. In any event, the wigs weren't made of real hair, and it was pretty obvious you were wearing one, so I opted to go without. I actually looked quite cool. I had a sort of Sinead O'Connor vibe going on. Of course, I was only young. I wouldn't like to try it now. These days, I'd have more of a Nosferatu vibe going on. Everybody, including Tom, kept slapping my head like Benny Hill used to do to his bald sidekick; I didn't get any sympathy. Smells could really nauseate me and I went off many different foods. I especially couldn't bear black pepper, or coffee. As the treatment progressed, I was pretty much surviving on Lucozade and cheesy Nik Naks, a knobbly maize snack. One day, I hadn't felt well so I stayed off work. Tom went in, but he drove home at lunchtime to check on me. He was immediately concerned and rang the doctor who arrived within the hour. All I remember was that my back was really hurting and the doctor gave me an injection. I was later told I was talking gibberish, but I don't remember that. An ambulance was called, and I was rushed to St Mary's with blue light and siren. The paramedic didn't stop talking. He kept firing questions at me. I remember thinking he was absolutely crap at his job. I was ill, and I really, really didn't want to talk. Of course I now know he was trying to prevent me from slipping into unconsciousness. I don't remember anything else.

I had Septicaemia. It was serious. The doctors said there was a real possibility I might die. If I survived the night, there was a good chance I would pull through. The whole family were summoned. It must have been a horribly long night for them. Sarah told me afterwards that Tom sobbed for most of the time. He couldn't pull himself together. But I made it, and I had the easy bit, as I don't remember a thing. I was given a blood transfusion which really bucked me up. For a while, I was put in isolation and had to be 'barrier nursed'. This meant that anyone who came into my room had to wear a full gown and face mask and visitors were restricted. Tom looked so funny in his gown. I was sent so many bouquets and many, many cards; none of which

I was permitted to have. The nurses stood in the corridor and held the flowers up at the window so I could see them, before whisking them away. I don't think it was so much my popularity as Tom's. People wanted to support him. I was worried about him driving. He would do a full day in the office, nip home to feed the cats, have a quick bite himself and then drive over to Portsmouth where he would stay until visiting time finished, a round trip of roughly forty miles. He did this every single day. He was so tired. He was beginning to look worse than me.

Eventually, I was moved back to the main ward where I had a room all to myself. Unbelievably in those days, we were allowed to smoke, and I had an ashtray by my bed. I smoked all through my treatment. The nurses bummed cigarettes from me constantly, most of them smoked. I had only been back in the main ward for a couple of days, when I developed Pleurisy. It was probably caused by my being immobile for so long. A nurse came every day and pummelled my back, like they do for people with cystic fibrosis. Still I smoked. The Pleurisy made it incredibly painful to inhale, but I persevered. I would manage a couple of puffs and then have to dock the cigarette. Five minutes later, I would relight the butt and try again. I was always pleased to have visitors as they brought me Lucozade and sweets, or sometimes grapes. The hospital food was horrendous. My theory is that the chefs didn't bother sending the decent grub to the cancer ward. They knew nobody had an appetite, and it would all come back untouched. I once ordered mac and cheese, and when I removed the cloche, I thought I had been given a plate of cashew nuts.

And then just as I was beginning to wonder how much more I could take, suddenly it was over. Almost a year after I had received my first treatment, I was told the chemotherapy appeared to have worked. I was in remission. On the day I was given the all clear, I saw Bob in the clinic. His Hodgkin's had spread to his bones and liver, and there was nothing more they could do. He asked how I got on, and I just couldn't bring myself to tell him my treatment had worked. I said I was waiting on some test results. I was heartbroken for him and his family; it was a bitter blow. I knew I had been very lucky. Had I got the disease just fifteen years earlier, it would have meant certain death. It was a sobering thought. Thankfully, nowadays

Hodgkin's Disease is one of the more treatable cancers. For the next five years, I would have to have regular check-ups. I was battered and bruised, but I had survived, and I was truly grateful. I hated feeling so unattractive, I wanted to hide away. I was still on a massive amount of steroids and had a great bloated face. When all is said and done however, it was a small price to pay. There are so many negative things about having cancer. The realisation that the disease could return at any time was an ever present worry. Suddenly you are aware that bad things can happen to you and those you love. I began to feel nervous about flying, thinking that because I was on board, the plane would be sure to crash. On the other hand, the whole ordeal makes you a better person. You realise that you are stronger than you ever thought possible. You have more empathy for other people's suffering. And never again will you feel suicidal over a bad haircut or a broken front tooth.

It felt good to be looking to the future again. Tom said once my hair started growing, we should get married.

Chapter 14
The Power of Love

My hair was growing. It came through much darker than before and very curly. I began to feel well again. It felt good to be young and alive. It felt good to party. There was some great music in the 1980s. Blondie, INXS, Tears for Fears, Duran Duran, OMD, Police, Tom Robinson, Men at Work, Dexy's Midnight Runners, Elvis Costello. These bands were the soundtrack to our lives. We wanted to get married as soon as possible, but we also wanted to do it cheaply. We were hoping to move at some stage as Tom was finding our kitchen too small. Neither of us liked being the centre of attention. If we could have had our way, we would have snuck off alone and tied the knot, but Tom knew it would break his mother's heart not to see him get married. It wouldn't have bothered my family at all. None of us liked weddings, which is surprising as between us, we've had so many. Sarah was about to be divorced for the second time. She and Martin remained firm friends; it was all very amicable. They both just realised they weren't suited. Sarah had decided to go to Israel and work on a kibbutz for a year, so she wouldn't be around when Tom and I got married.

I went with Tom to choose an engagement ring. I picked a classic trinity ring of three matched diamonds in a row. It was beautiful, I couldn't stop looking at my hand. I was incredibly happy. Dawn accompanied me to Winchester to buy my wedding outfit. I eventually found a Laura Ashley dress in heavy cotton. It was a rich violet mauve, floor length with a fitted bodice and flared skirt. It had a large bow at the back and puffed sleeves. I had little cream leather pumps, cream lace gloves and a cream fascinator with a lace veil which covered half my face. Dawn said I looked gorgeous, and I seem to remember I was quite pleased with the outfit at the time. However, looking at my wedding photos now, I looked like a bit of a prat. We got married on July 10 at the Register Office in Bishop's Waltham, just down the road from Swanmore. We had a barbecue reception held in Godfrey and Jane's large back garden. The gods smiled on us that day. It was a really hot, and we all stayed in the garden until past 2 am. The champagne was flowing, and all our friends were there. I'm pleased to report that we also had a beautiful cake. One friend was a butcher, and he and his wife gave us a whole lamb to spit roast as a wedding present. Tom loved that lamb; he was never away from it. He spent all morning setting up the spit then marinating the meat and rubbing spices into it. Then he spent all afternoon turning the spit and basting. When he wasn't doing something to the meat, he was busy tending the fire. Several people commented that for a moment, they thought Tom was going to marry the lamb. They had a point; it certainly received more love and attention than me that day. I didn't mind. It was good to see him so happy. It had been a fabulous wedding. Wearily we fell into our marital bed. We were both too tired to make love. Maybe that was an omen.

A couple of weeks later, we were off to Spain. This time we drove. It was so much better than flying. We had a proper berth on the overnight ferry. There was a bit of a hiccough and a few cross words when I left my handbag in the toilet overnight with the passports inside. Luckily, someone handed the bag in, and nothing was missing. But it did mean we had to forego breakfast, and Tom could be very sour when hungry. But we were soon friends again, speeding along in Tom's GTI, Dire Straits playing loudly on the cd. Perfect. We broke the journey up by staying overnight in one of Spain's national hotels or Paradors. They are stunningly beautiful, often old historical buildings such as monasteries and castles. Tom was very happy to see our room had two single beds. I could read his mind. For once, I wasn't too bothered. My sex drive had taken a bit of a nosedive. My face was still slightly puffy, and my hair was very short, I didn't feel desirable. So long as we had plenty of cuddles, which we did, I was happy. We had a wonderful time. It was so good to see Nerja again. This time, we rented our own apartment, still in El Capistrano but nearer the sea. Because we had the car, we purchased a lot of booze and other bits and bobs. We bought a huge oil painting; it only just fitted in the car with the back seats down. It was very expensive. Tom had to use two different cards to pay for it, but we couldn't resist. We also bought a timeshare. The more I got to know Tom, the more I realised he was incapable of saying no. Unless of course it was to sex. Anything else, he just couldn't do it. He was a sales person's dream. On our first trip to Spain, I had nipped to the loo, and when I got back, he had bought a large rug from a 'lookie lookie' man. It wasn't even nice. He loved watching QVC, mainly the presentations on kitchen equipment and household gadgets. As the presenter started piling on pressure, saying, "You need to hurry folks, stocks are running low," Tom took on a bit of a worried look, and I knew he was wrestling with himself. As soon as the words "We're down to the last hundred" had left the presenter's lips, Tom would be dialling. So I knew that it was inevitable that once the timeshare rep had expended all of ten seconds persuading Tom to attend the presentation, we would be leaving with a time share. And I was right.

Timeshares have had a bad press, which is probably more to do with the way they are sold than the actual product. Ours ended up working out well. We bought a two-week peak timeshare in a new villa in El Capistrano. It was five-star accommodation with a private pool and a breath-taking view. If we didn't use our two weeks, we could 'pool' them which meant we could have double time the next year. If we swapped for a destination out of Europe, we also got double time. If for some reason we didn't use our weeks, we sold them to friends at mate's rates, and it made us a nice bit of money. We soon recouped our initial outlay. There was a yearly maintenance charge, but it was negligible. Our holiday was over all too soon, and we began the long drive home. On the return journey, I found myself wishing we had flown. Once the holiday is over, you just want to get home as quickly as possible. Our suitcases were full of dirty clothes, and we were already contemplating our return to work. Coming through customs at Portsmouth, we were made to completely unpack our car. The customs officer gave Tom a right grilling, questioning him on what route we had taken, which towns we had passed through and where we had stayed. We actually began to believe we were guilty of something. I would absolutely love to work for customs. Making people unpack their luggage, holding up dirty underwear and putting dildos through the x-ray machine. Maybe slashing a few Louis Vuitton case linings. Oh the power. It was with great relief that we eventually made it home.

We had only been back for a couple of days and were in bed when the phone rang. Although it was after midnight, this wasn't unusual. Tom had to take a turn being the duty solicitor in case someone was arrested and needed legal advice. I always felt rather sorry for the poor schmuck in the cells who got Tom, unless of course they wanted to buy a house. His knowledge of criminal law was sketchy at best. This particular night, he wasn't on call, but if the police couldn't get hold of whoever was on duty, they might try Tom. Or it meant that the alarm had tripped at his office, and the police wanted the key holder. However, when Tom answered, it was Danny. He said, "I know where you live," and hung up. We were concerned, but there was nothing we could do. As it happened that would be the last either of us ever heard from Danny, so we needn't have worried.

For quite a while, we had been thinking of moving. We needed more space, and Tom especially wanted a bigger kitchen. Just down the road from Swanmore is the medieval market town of Bishop's Waltham. It was where we had recently married. Tom noticed there was a new development of executive houses being built by Bovis on a piece of land which had previously been used to grow Christmas trees. We decided to go and look at the show home. It was absolutely beautiful. Quite a lot of the plots had already been sold, but one that was still available immediately caught our eye. It was a four bedroom detached with a double garage. It was a corner plot, and the fact that the house was so wide, meant the back garden was big. Tom quickly arranged the mortgage. We had found our new home.

It seemed to take forever for the house to be built. Every weekend we donned our wellies and trudged through the sea of mud to see what progress there had been. As the building neared completion, and we could actually walk around inside, our excitement grew. The house was a design called 'the Chatsworth' and was one of three being constructed on the estate. Once more, we had the corner house in a small cul-de-sac. All the houses were detached. Three of them were larger five bedroom properties. Being on a corner, our house had by far the biggest garden. Eventually, it was finished. Before moving we had the carpet fitted. It was steel blue/grey with a pile so deep you could lose things in it. The same carpet ran throughout the house. There was a large square hall with downstairs toilet off a study, dining room and lounge. The lounge had a real fireplace and double patio doors opening onto the garden. The kitchen was huge. There was a big double oven and a separate gas hob. A small utility room housed the gas boiler. A path ran from the back door to the double garage. Upstairs there were four bedrooms, one with en-suite and a bathroom. The windows throughout were leaded. All the inside timber was dark stained, but we planned to change this to white when we decorated. It was a beautiful house. So, with a fair amount of sadness we said goodbye to our home in Swanmore and moved to Bishop's Waltham. And that night, we christened our new king size bed.

We had acquired another kitten, a Havana Brown. She looked like a Siamese, but instead of being white, her coat was the colour of a Red Setter dog, or a newly fallen conker. We named her Cleo. Because we had the five cats, getting the back garden turfed was a priority. Otherwise, we would have had a very muddy house. Unfortunately, that meant we didn't have time to improve the drainage and enrich the soil before laying the turf. Consequently, the resulting lawn was more moss and weeds than grass, but it was green, and it looked fine if Tom cut it regularly. Within a year, we had decorated the entire house and painted the brown woodwork white. It made the whole place look larger and lighter. We had curtains and blinds made to measure and new light fittings in every room. Tom's colleague Nick had given us an old 1930s' sofa. It had a solid beech frame and the cushions still had their original horsehair stuffing. It weighed a ton. We had it re-upholstered in a lovely soft grey linen. The upholsterer also added casters so it was easier to move. We began collecting limited edition prints and had acquired several original paintings. We hung the one we had brought from Spain in the dining room. Soon there wasn't a bare wall in the house. We both spent too much. Tom was earning really good money, but we never put any of it by for a rainy day. We thought the good times would last forever. The banks were falling over themselves to extend Tom's credit. He had a platinum MasterCard and a gold American Express, and we spent liberally on both. Tom had several insurance policies and a good pension, so we didn't worry. He paid for all the household bills and for the main weekly shop. My salary was used for anything extra. He had sold his Peugeot GTI and now had a Toyota supplied by the partnership. He was still really busy at work, and it seemed our life really couldn't get much better.

I became gardening mad. I couldn't pass a garden centre. Every weekend, I would drive out to a nearby nursery and return with my car packed with plants to be added to the sweeping herbaceous border which ran the entire length of the garden. I planted trees and bushes along the back to give height and hide the fence. The boundary nearest the road was a brick wall and against this, I planted honeysuckle and clematis. The flowerbed at the base of the wall was shady, and this became my fernery. Amongst the ferns, I planted Solomon's Seal, Dicentra, Hostas and white Foxgloves. We had a large pond built. It was circular, twelve feet in diameter and three feet deep. I had read in a book that the larger the pond, the better the water quality as the temperature doesn't fluctuate as much. This means there is less of a problem with algae and blanket weed. Our pond was crystal clear. We added water lilies, pond weed a variety of marginal plants and a few fish. Before long, the pond was teeming with frogs, newts and aquatic insects. As spring turned to summer, vast numbers of electric blue damselflies flitted over the water vying for airspace with fluorescent green dragonflies which swooped about like mini helicopters. The same contractor who had built the pond made us a flagstone patio. A little raised wall ran along most of its edge, and into this, I planted brightly-coloured alpines and trailing plants, dotting crocus and snowdrop bulbs in between them ready for Spring.

If I was hooked on gardening, Tom had been well and truly bitten by the cookery bug. He had always been a good cook but in the past had mostly stuck to English dishes like roasts, casseroles and shepherd's pie. He made everything from scratch. He didn't even buy mayonnaise. He became a devotee of Indian cuisine, grinding all his own spices and making the most wonderful curries. He prided himself on having any spice you could name in his cupboard. The smell when the cupboard door was opened was wonderful. He also adored cooking Chinese and Thai. We would drive to the Eastern Stores in Southsea and come home laden with goodies. Bags of lime and curry leaves, tamarind, fresh roots of turmeric and ginger and great bunches of musty smelling coriander. At night, we would lie in bed, Tom, with Madhur Jaffrey, me with Alan Titchmarsh, happy in our own little bubbles.

Chapter 15
Fool You've Landed

September came around, and once again, we were heading for Spain. This time we were going with a couple of friends. Our villa comfortably slept up to six people, so there was plenty of room. We mostly went out as a foursome, but occasionally, Tom and I went off on our own. One night we were in a restaurant, just the two of us, when we were suddenly surrounded by a trio of enthusiastic Spaniards in national dress, strumming guitars and singing *O Sole Mio*. Quite why they were singing in Italian is a mystery. Perhaps they were Italians posing as Spaniards, or maybe they just liked the song. Whatever, it was all mighty embarrassing. I didn't know whether to join in, clap along or just carry on eating. Tom sat fork poised in mid-air, staring at his plate. I think the musicians thoroughly enjoyed our discomfort. I'm pretty sure they sang the whole song twice. Either that or they were waiting for a tip, in which case they were very disappointed.

Next day, we all went to the beach. Tom wanted to have a go at water skiing. The men had been taking people out all morning. Young kids were performing backflips and skiing on one leg whilst writing postcards and waving cheerily to their parents. It looked easy enough. Poor Tom, I don't think he ever broke the surface of the water. A couple of times we caught a fleeting glimpse of a blue bottom, but he was basically towed under water for the whole ten minutes. He emerged coughing and sputtering and very pissed off. It gave me a good laugh though. Throughout the holiday, Tom didn't seem to have a care in the world. But he did keep nipping off to the phone box, sometimes several times a day. He said he was just keeping tabs on things at the office which was totally feasible. I knew he hated delegating work to anyone else. It was hard even getting him to take a holiday. I didn't give it a second thought.

Back home, Tom seemed absolutely normal. On Monday, we both returned to work. That evening, we had just finished our meal when Tom said, "I've got something to tell you. I've been booted out of the partnership." It transpired that he had lent £40,000 of the firm's money to an acquaintance who used it for a deposit on a property and then couldn't get the funds to complete. If you exchange contracts but don't complete, the seller can charge interest and ultimately you forfeit the deposit. The chap who had taken the money had been introduced to Tom by a broker who had a very dodgy reputation. Both the client and the broker had told Tom that there would be no trouble raising the purchase monies. They had asked Tom if he would arrange a bridging loan. Tom knew full well that you never exchange contracts without a firm mortgage offer in writing. He knew it was wrong, but he couldn't say no. Thankfully, it was firm's money. If it had been money from the firm's client account, Tom would have been struck off and probably gone to prison. As it was, several of the partners wanted Tom to be dismissed, but Steven stuck up for him. Also, the fact that Tom earned the firm such enormous profits counted in his favour. He would however be removed from Gosport office and would come to work at Fareham as a salaried solicitor. He would also have to be supervised, and all his files overseen by Steven.

Tom had known the shit had hit the fan all the time we were in Spain, but he had shown no sign that anything was wrong. Even now, he didn't seem bothered in the least. Over the next few days, his car was taken away and his name was removed from the list of partners on the firm's headed paper. He was now listed as an assistant solicitor in the tiniest of print. The office at Gosport was shut down, and all the staff relocated to Fareham. Once again, I would be sharing an office with Tom. Three big local firms approached Tom. Such was his popularity and reputation as a money maker; all three offered him an immediate partnership if he would join them. I wanted Tom to salvage some pride and take up the offer, but he refused to even consider it. I was furious with him, and I was so disappointed. I felt devastated about his demotion. I had been so proud that he was a partner. I loved being the wife of a partner and all it entailed. Of course, I was quite wrong. I had nothing to be proud about. I wasn't a partner. I hadn't earned it. I should have supported Tom, but all I could think of was what we would lose and how I was going to face people. I suddenly saw Tom as weak and gullible. And I had another reason to be bitter and full of disappointment. Following the chemotherapy, my periods hadn't resumed. A test now confirmed that at the ripe old age twenty-eight, I was going through the menopause. There would be no children for us. Nowadays before commencing chemotherapy you can have your eggs frozen, but it wasn't an option then. In any event, there is no way on this earth Tom would have gone into a small hospital room and produced a sample of sperm. Even if he did agree, a girly mag wouldn't have helped him rise to the occasion, although, Good Housekeeping might have done the trick.

Tom settled well into Fareham office; the secretaries all loved him. He was soon busier than ever. He was strictly forbidden to have any contact with the broker who had caused all the trouble, but he took absolutely no notice and continued to take both his calls and his business. Steven would storm into Tom's office and give him a real carpeting, which affected Tom not one jot. I was now working for another one of the partners, an older man called Mike. Almost every secretary in the office had worked for him at some time; he went through secretaries like a dose of salts. Most refused to ever work for him again. He could be incredibly bad tempered and demanding. He abhorred sloppy work and bad spelling in particular. He did a lot of court work which involved preparing large bundles of papers for Counsel. Accuracy was essential, and luckily, I was both an accurate typist and a fast one. My spelling wasn't bad either, and if I couldn't spell a word, I would always look it up. Mike and I made an unlikely partnership, but he became very fond of me, and we became friends. I loved working for him because he took on a bit of everything. Criminal work, probate, accident claims. It was interesting. I did occasionally get a ticking off. You knew there was trouble when he would buzz your phone and say, "Let's have a chat." I dreaded those words. Most of our 'chats' were over my days off sick. My lupus was bad again, particularly my hands. Mike hated my being away as no one else ever wanted to help him out. The other girls would all suddenly be too busy, and to be fair, they probably were. It was hard for people to understand how ill I was because when they did see me, I looked totally fine. I would explain that I had had a bad flare up, and they would look at me suspiciously and say, "What brought that on then?" As if I had done something to cause it. Sometimes, when I came back to work after a couple of days' sick, I could sense the rather frosty atmosphere with the other girls. Just as our life was regaining its equilibrium, Rasputin was killed on the road outside our house. We came across his body one morning. About a month later, Sammy was also killed. Whoever hit him, put an anonymous note through our door saying, "I'm sorry, I hit your cat, and he ran into the bushes." It took Tom a long time to find his little body; he was lying deep in a thicket of brambles. We buried Raz and Sam in the garden and planted a Magnolia tree in remembrance. From that moment on, we locked the cat flap at night to stop them from going out. That same year, we had Ricky put to sleep. He had lived a long and happy life, and we buried him alongside Razzy and Sam.

Tom continued to be irresponsible, or maybe I was just starting to notice it more. He would regularly let people down. Usually this could be attributed to his inability to say no. One particular morning, we were woken really early by the doorbell. I answered and was amazed to see a taxi outside full of his friends. They were happy and excited and had called to collect Tom to go on holiday. He hadn't bothered to let them know he wouldn't be going. They had even been discussing the arrangements in the pub the night before. Another time, I answered the phone at home, and it was a mate who said, "Where are you?" Apparently, Tom had accepted an invitation for us to stay with them at their home in Bath that weekend. He hadn't bothered to tell me or to cancel with them. It drove me mad, and it caused a lot of rows. The thing was, everybody always forgave Tom. Nobody ever stayed mad at him, and I think that was part of the problem. Tom's propensity let people down was looked on as one of his little foibles. On the other hand, he had many good things about him. He loved animals. In the summer, each evening as dusk approached, we would make our way to an upstairs window and watch the bats perform their aerial ballet over our back garden. Tom was transfixed; he never tired of the spectacle. We were also both delighted when we realised we had hedgehogs in the garden. We would open a window and hear them snuffling and crashing around in the flower border. They aren't exactly stealthy. I suppose it's because they don't have any natural predators, unless you count gypsies of course. One day, Tom drove all the way home from work in his lunch break with a stag beetle he had found on the pavement. He was worried someone would tread on it and had put it in his sandwich box with some leaves and grass. He had even named him 'Staggery'. Tom also loved birds. We had several bird boxes on the side of the house. One box was used every year by a pair of blue tits to raise their large brood. I remember once driving through our estate and seeing a man actually using a pressure hose to remove the little mud nests made by swifts from the wall of his house. Arsehole. Tom put up five bird feeders, and these were filled with either seed or peanuts. He topped them up every day; they were never allowed to run out. All our trees were hung with fat balls. In the morning, before the cats were allowed out, he put down food for the ground feeders. He got through a huge amount of bird food; some of the feeders were really big. He would order the feed in bulk, and it came in massive brown sacks which he had delivered to the office. Reception was constantly filled with sacks of bird food. Clients would have to weave their way between them to get to where they were going. Steven was always complaining and telling Tom it had to stop, but the sacks kept coming.

Tom was wonderfully kind. He knew how badly the lupus affected me and how much I suffered. He did the lion's share of the housework, all the hoovering and cleaning of bathrooms and kitchen. Every Saturday morning, he did the weekly shop. If I needed to go anywhere that wasn't local, he would drop me off and pick me up. He never once said, "You've got a car. You drive." He took me to all my hospital appointments, which often involved waiting around for hours. I can only remember him moaning once and that was when he parked in a restricted area and got clamped. He also didn't turn into a slob the way Danny had done. He wouldn't have dreamt of taking even a pee in front of me, the toilet door was always very firmly shut. He never swore, and he never smelt bad.

So as the eighties wound to a close, we were hopeful that our run of bad luck was behind us.

Chapter 16
Everybody's Changing

As we entered the 1990s, our lives began to change. Tom had always been sporty. He occasionally still played hockey for the veterans. In the summer, he played a fair bit of cricket. He was a brilliant cricketer and was always in high demand with local teams. He was asked not to play at a small pitch in Swanmore because he kept hitting the ball out of the grounds. Several residents living nearby had complained about their houses or cars being hit, and it was nearly always Tom. One couple in the pub across the road had a narrow escape when Tom hit a ball out of the cricket ground and straight through the pub window. I think Tom was quite proud. He drove by to show me the window, and there was a perfect round hole in the glass, exactly the size of a cricket ball. He was a member of a nearby country club where he played squash, and for a time, he was their best player. He was always in the club's top league. He now took up golf and soon became obsessed. He had taken golf lessons as a youngster and had been a good player then. He soon rediscovered his previous good form and at his best had a handicap of six. As the years went by, his handicap slipped to eight but that is still pretty good (so I'm told). I, on the other hand, have no interest whatsoever in sport, either in taking part or as a spectator. Part of the reason is because I had asthma in childhood, but mainly it's because I am a seriously bad loser. I was the person who, if I saw someone about to pass me in a race, would trip over a blade of grass and hurl myself to the ground with a twisted ankle. Over the years, I have tipped up more Monopoly boards then I would care to mention. I take it particularly badly if I am playing with a gloater. In family games, Sarah would invariably own the whole side of the board beginning with The Strand and ending with Mayfair and Park Lane. Mother never quite got the hang of things and would actively try to buy Old Kent Road and Whitechapel because they sounded like pretty places to live. I would end up with something mediocre like Vine Street or The Angel Islington. Whatever I did own, Sarah would sail by every round, pausing only momentarily to land on 'chance' and collect ten pounds for winning a beauty contest. Or, it would be her birthday, and we would all have to stump up ten pounds, which I did very begrudgingly. When it was my turn, without fail, I would land on Mayfair with a hotel. Sarah would make a great show of consulting her little property card, just the hint of a smirk playing at the corner of her mouth and proceed to clean me out. It never failed to cause me to have a meltdown. I don't know why I ever agreed to play. I hated that damn game. Nanny once took Sarah and me to the Isle of Wight on holiday. The hotel had a crazy golf course, and we played a lot. There was one particular hole which I just could not do. Sarah would chip the ball in neatly and be on to the next hole, but I would be stuck, sometimes for what seemed like hours. Sarah would often lap me. By then, I would be apoplectic with rage and frustration. Sarah would say, "You can give that hole a miss if you can't do it." Again, I would catch that flicker of a smile by which time, I had slung my club and stomped off back to the hotel. I don't know why I was such a bad loser. I always lost. I lost so often, I should have been used to it. It's something I'm not proud of, but it is a fact.

With Tom's love of golf growing almost daily, he began to mix with a new crowd. Mainly these were all keen golfers. He started to drop all his old friends. If you didn't play golf, he wasn't interested. I had loved our group of friends. I loved their wives and girlfriends. With Tom's new crowd, the men mostly socialised together whilst the wives stayed at home with the children. I had nothing in common with them. A couple of the men were notorious womanisers, and this was tolerated, even applauded. Their behaviour could be laddish. I got the feeling that once again Tom was being easily led.

Our menagerie had grown. We had two rabbits and eleven guinea pigs. The rabbits each had their own individual hutches in the garage where they would sleep at night. During the day, they ran free in the garden. Each night, Tom would have to round them up and drive them back into the garage. He had so much patience. Sometimes he would just get them to the garage door when they would scoot through his legs back out into the garden. He would have to begin shepherding them all over again. I would have said, "Sod you then, you can stay out," and stalked back indoors, but Tom never minded how long it took him to get the rabbits in. The guinea pigs had a huge run also in the garage (our large double garage never saw a car). When the weather was nice, Tom would make the guinea pigs an outdoor run using several chicken wire panels tied together with string. He loved constructing the runs making them more and more elaborate, sometimes encompassing large parts of the flower border. He would move the guinea pigs between runs loading them into a couple of wire shopping baskets, five in one and six in the other. I remember having to take two of the guinea pigs to the vet for their claws to be clipped, something minor. Whilst the vet was busy with one guinea pig, Tom held the other to his chest and kept planting great smacking kisses on its head. I'm not sure he was even aware he was doing it. We had gone straight from work so what the vet made of this great big man in suit and tie cuddling a guinea pig and repeatedly kissing it, I can't imagine. Tom also had four big aquariums. The one in the lounge was a tropical community tank. There was another tank in the study which was home to two large catfish, and also in the study was a brackish tank with cichlids and bumblebee gobies. In the kitchen was a big cold water aquarium, which was my favourite. Tom kept all the tanks to the highest standard. They all contained real plants, and the fish looked happy and healthy.

Because we had so many animals, we stopped going away together on holiday. Tom had several golfing holidays with the men. They usually went either to Spain or the USA. Wives and girlfriends were never invited. As a couple, we still went out regularly. In the mid 1980s, we had seen Queen at Wembley on 'The Works' tour. Tom absolutely loved them. Freddie Mercury died in 1991, so I am so glad I got to see them again. We also saw Dire Straits twice, and they were fantastic. We often ate out and went to the theatre or cinema. Tom had got tickets to see Dame Edna Everidge in London with two friends. We were all looking forward to it; the reviews were excellent. Just a few days before the show, I contracted shingles. It got really bad quite quickly. The blisters were all down one side of my face and spread to the inside of my mouth. I was too poorly to go to see the show in London so the three of them went without me. Because shingles is so painful, the GP prescribed me Dihydrocodeine a strong opioid painkiller, often used post-operatively. When I was with Danny, his friends occasionally got hold of them. They always referred to them as DF118's. Almost the minute I swallowed the tablets, the pain from the shingles vanished and so did the pain from my lupus. It was like wonderful magic, all that pain just melted away. Suddenly, I no longer felt I could happily cut my hands off each night. I could move about without wanting to cry. About twenty minutes after taking the two pills, I would experience an amazing high. I felt lively and chatty, like I used to when I took amphetamine. Unfortunately for me, it was a feeling I loved. The shingles was gone, but I continued taking the codeine. I kept renewing my repeat prescription, and when those pills had gone, I put in for another. Soon I was no longer leaving the required four hours between doses; I took two tablets every two hours. Once two hours had passed, I felt slightly agitated and out of sorts until I had the next lot of pills. I failed to see what was staring me in the face. I was fast becoming addicted. Whilst I was grappling with the codeine, Tom had a slight medical problem of his own. A mole on his back had started to weep and itch. Because I read a lot of women's magazines, I was quite clued up on the importance of checking moles, and I persuaded him to see his doctor. The doctor wasn't concerned, but he referred Tom to the hospital to have the mole removed. It was done in a jiffy. Tom had a couple of small stitches, and we thought no more about it.

We had been arguing a lot about our lack of a sex life. It had dwindled to maybe once a month, if I nagged. You often hear people say they fall asleep the minute their head hits the pillow. With Tom, this was absolutely true. It never ceased to amaze me how quickly he could go from being wide awake to comatose. It was instantaneous. Exactly like when a hypnotist clicks his fingers and says 'sleep' only with Tom the trigger word was 'sex'. I just could not accept that he had such a low sex drive. Because of my own low self-esteem, I put it down to my being unattractive, and I couldn't cope with that thought. Tom told me time and time again that it wasn't about me. He told me time and time again that he loved me more than anything in the world, but without the physical manifestation of love, I felt like nothing.

When we fought, usually at night, I wouldn't let it go. I went on and on and on at him. Sometimes, we would both be exhausted and desperately in need of sleep. Every time Tom put the bedroom light out, I would switch it back on. I was like some evil torturer of old using sleep deprivation, only I was depriving both of us. All I wanted was for Tom to say, "Come on, let's stop this," and just hug me. Of course, at that precise moment, he was more likely closer to hating me. I had a real issue coping with rejection. I couldn't handle it, and in my mind, Tom was rejecting me. I'm no psychiatrist, but I think it's all part and parcel of hating to lose. It feels the same, being second best, being inferior. Occasionally, it crossed my mind that Tom may have been abused at boarding school. It was a draconian regime. He once told me that they had to take cold baths in the mornings to toughen them up, strengthen their characters. I'm sorry, but only a pervert and a sadist would make small boys sit in cold water at any time of day. Sometimes I wondered if he was latently gay. Probably the real reason was that our relationship had subtly changed. I had gradually become more like Tom's mother than his wife. Also, I believe the adage 'familiarity breeds contempt'. There was still a lot of love between us, but we weren't in love. I had all too often let my disappointment in Tom show, and it had emasculated him. Or maybe, what I feared most was true. He just didn't fancy me. Although it was never discussed, my inability to have children made me feel like a great big failure. I had always struggled with not feeling like a proper woman. I often felt I was stuck in a time warp, unable to grow up emotionally. We had reached an age when most of our friends were starting families, and although I never let it show, it was tough. Tom said he didn't want kids anyway, but whether that was just for my benefit, I'll never know. I have to say, we wouldn't have made good parents. We both had way too many issues; we were both flawed. It was probably a good thing that we didn't pass on our genes.

We still had fun. We loved cooking together, and we loved our animals. Cats, Oliver and Cleo had been joined by three Devon Rexes. Morph and Gizmo were brothers who we bought as kittens. Star was also a Devon Rex from the same breeder. She was a year old when we got her. She was white and looked like an explosion in a cotton wool factory but with a little bald neck and tummy. She had a funny little tooth which stuck out from her bottom lip at a right-angle. Every Sunday, we would cook a large joint or a turkey and share it with the cats. Tom loved them all milling round whilst he threw bits of meat to each cat in turn, making sure they all got a fair share. It was his favourite part of Sunday lunchtime. If we were at home, Tom always cooked the Sunday roast. We still went to Godfrey and Jane's for lunch at least once a month. During the week, I cooked. As soon as he got home from work, Tom would stroll into the village and meet his buddies in the pub for a quick drink. By the time he got home, dinner would be ready. He was such a pleasure to cook for; he really loved his grub and would tuck in with gusto. One of the only times you would see Tom in a mood was if he had a bad meal. If a curry or chilli was advertised as being hot and wasn't, he would sulk. Or, if he was hungry. In either scenario, he would be totally miserable and would moan at length. Food really mattered to him.

Chapter 17
Comfortably Numb

I was in the grip of a serious addiction. I was taking six 30mg tablets at a time, every four hours. I'm not going to do the maths, but that's a lot of codeine. I couldn't do without the pills; the withdrawal was awful. Heroin addicts refer to it as 'rattling', and it's a fair description. Every single nerve in your body feels out of sorts. Your nose runs, you feel like you're going to lose control of your bowels, you can't sleep, but you can't stay awake either. It is totally true that you would do absolutely anything, just to get more drugs to enable you to feel normal again. You quickly lose the delicious high that so hooked you in the first place. You just need the drugs to function. I was still putting in repeat prescriptions two or three times a week. I used several different chemists to get them dispensed, but I knew it was only a matter of time before someone at the doctor's surgery noticed how many requests I was putting in. I made an appointment and confessed all to my GP. I think he was pretty horrified that I had been submitting so many repeat prescriptions for so long. The practice quickly reviewed their repeat prescription procedure. We agreed that I would try to cut down on the pills. He would prescribe me a week's worth at a time, steadily decreasing. It was a plan but not a good one. I started visiting GP's all over Hampshire. I would book in under a false name saying that I was in the area on holiday. I would give a home address in Canada and a local bed and breakfast or hotel as a temporary residence. Because I had lupus, I would always request my lupus medication first and then add as an afterthought, "Oh, I take Dihydrocodeine for pain, and I'm running a bit low. Could I have some more of those please." It worked like a charm every single time.

The sad thing is I didn't want to stop. I loved those small

white tablets. I would sit up late into the night, smoking and popping pills, devouring my gardening books whilst Tom snored softly beside me. Anybody who has ever taken codeine will know that it causes terrible constipation. It's no lie to say that I only had a bowel movement every two to three weeks. And I was still eating three meals a day. I was literally full of shit. When I did go, it resembled the droppings of a giant rabbit—great big hard balls. It wasn't good, but it wasn't enough to make me want to stop. Once in a blue moon, the pharmacist would get my prescription wrong and give me double the amount of pills. When this happened, I felt like I had won the lottery. I was whooping and punching the air. When my bottle of pills was full, I was happy. As it started to empty, I started to feel stressed, knowing that somehow I had to get more. Around this time, I made friends with a girl at work called Vivienne. She was fourteen years younger than me, but we got on like a house on fire. She was incredibly witty, and I love people who can make me laugh. We were similar in many ways. She also had a rather dysfunctional family and a history of drug taking. Currently her drug of choice was alcohol. It's fair to say she was a functioning alcoholic. She only ever drank wine, but she drank a bottle every night. All she ever ate was pizza. My sister Sarah was back from the kibbutz having returned with a new boyfriend and a large dog. She had met David on the kibbutz, and they had quickly become an item. He was lovely, a real clown. He reminded me of a big friendly puppy. He was super enthusiastic about everything and bounced around playing the fool. You wouldn't have thought he had an ounce of sense, but in fact, he had a maths degree and was a computer whizz. Shortly after returning from Israel, they bought a cottage in Haslemere and set up their own IT consultancy, working from home. It wasn't long before David had some choice London contracts. The dog, Socks, was a stray they had adopted on the kibbutz. When their time was up, they obviously couldn't leave him so they paid a small fortune to have him flown to Britain and quarantined for six months. By the time I had got pally with Vivienne, they had been back from Israel for over a year and had taken on a little mongrel dog called Pepper. Now they were off to Canada on holiday, and I had offered to dog sit. Vivienne was coming too.

Tom drove us both to Haslemere. We were like a couple of

excited kids. To be honest, we weren't good for each other at all. It's hard to say who was the worse influence, but I suppose I must put my hand up, as I was so much older. The minute Tom had left, Vivienne unpacked her wine box, and I unpacked my pill bottles. She had also brought a good supply of cannabis. I hadn't touched dope since I had been with Danny, but of course I took back to it like a duck to water. Sarah had left us the keys to her car, so we could take the dogs to the nearby forest for their walks. We were in Haslemere for two whole weeks, and we never once managed to find reverse. It took quite a bit of creativity and route planning to avoid having to ever go backwards. I don't know how we managed, but we did. Most of the holiday was spent visiting all the GP surgeries in Haslemere and the surrounding area to keep me in codeine. The only other time we ventured out (other than dog walks) was to the co-op just down the road for Rizlas, cigarettes, wine and frozen pizza. The co-op must have been surprised and delighted to have such a sudden upturn in pizza sales. They had probably just tripled their usual order when it was time for us to go home. The manager is probably still scratching his head, wondering why the great pizza boon ended so suddenly. By the time Tom collected us at the end of two weeks, we were red-eyed, spotty-faced and greasy-haired. We had the pallor of the dead, and we reeked of dog. I could see Tom was not best pleased. He totally blamed Vivienne for leading me astray. If only he knew. Back home, our friendship continued. I would often stay over at hers on a Friday night. We would get absolutely smashed together and have a high old time. It was like being a teenager again.

Money had become tight for pretty much everyone. Interest rates rose sharply, and many people with mortgages found themselves in negative equity. One friend of ours who had recently bought a brand new five-bedroom property with his wife, just handed the keys back to the building society and moved out. They had to go back to living with his parents. Our monthly mortgage payment was huge. We had to get rid of one of our cars, and Tom cashed in nearly all his insurance policies. Times were hard. All of a sudden, we couldn't afford the little treats we were used to. Tom's flexible friend was no longer so flexible. The only thing Tom didn't cut back on was our food shopping. He spent a small fortune at the local butcher's each week. The butcher's eyes positively lit up when he spotted Tom and his cheque book heading on in. It was the same in the greengrocers. He bought a huge amount of fruit and veg. Our animal food bill was also pretty steep. Where we could, we would buy in bulk. Clients now had to step over bales of straw as well as bird feed when they came to the office.

My codeine consumption continued unchecked. I was also becoming extremely depressed. I missed a lot of days at work which was making me unpopular with the girls who had to cover for me and with Mike and Steven. I didn't want to get up in the mornings. The only time I was happy was when I was swallowing tablets or getting stoned with Vivienne. My lupus was extremely active, and my fingers had started to drift slightly sideways. I cried at the slightest thing; mentally I was on a knife edge. I didn't want to be bothered with anything. Tom was hopeless when it came to depression. He had no understanding of the condition whatsoever. He just expected me to buck myself up. We didn't ever talk, only about the animals or cooking. It was all small talk, and I needed so much more. I always knew he was quiet but assumed him to be deep and interesting. Now I was beginning to think he was just plain boring. We were never intimate. I had completely given up even trying. His assets had frozen and mine had dropped. I felt so ugly anyway it was the last thing on my mind. Our relationship had become platonic. Eventually, I went back to the doctor, and he put me on a strict regime of collecting my tablets daily. It was horrible. I would take my last dose in the evening and would wake up next morning in withdrawal until I could get to the chemist to pick up my day's script. I never got washed or dressed to go into the village. I would put my coat on over my night clothes and shuffle off to the chemist. Once I had taken my morning dose, all was well with the world, but soon the cycle would begin all over again. Just when we most needed the money, I gave up my job. I wasn't fit to work anymore. Tom was okay, he didn't have much choice, but it put additional strain on our already fragile relationship.

Because I was so depressed and so codeine dependent, I was admitted into the nearby psychiatric hospital for ten days. The idea was to get me stabilised on a methadone programme. That way I would avoid the constant coming up and down that is associated with opioid use. My goodness, that hospital was an eye-opener. It was an old almost gothic Victorian building, oppressive and haunting. You just knew that within those forbidding walls, there had been a whole lot of screaming. Even the grounds appeared menacing, full of dark, brooding conifers and yew trees. Some of the patients there were really mixed up. One young girl wouldn't be parted from a life-size baby doll. Another young woman had been sexually abused for years by her own brother. There were several inmates on round the clock suicide watch. Of course, I got on well with most of them. They were damaged like me. We whiled away the hours chatting and chain-smoking, but it was all pretty grim. Almost every day someone would try to storm the drugs trolley when the nurse was dispensing the medication. It was quite a highlight. We all secretly hoped someone would have a go. I think it even livened up the nurses' day. There were a couple of alcoholics with end stage liver disease and that wasn't pretty. One elderly lady had dementia, and every time Tom visited, she would appear stumping along the corridor with her Zimmer frame, completely naked. Tom didn't know where to look. All in all, I was one of the more normal patients. I had to be taken off to a little side room to be given the methadone. It was bright green and horribly sweet, but it certainly worked. It kept you from going into withdrawal without giving you the high. After I had served my time, I was released. I would have to get my methadone from our village pharmacy daily, until I could be trusted to be given a weeks' supply at once. Some pharmacies insist you drink the methadone on the premises in their presence, but I was allowed to take mine away.

Before I went into hospital, no one had thought to take back the Dihydrocodeine I already had in my possession, and I had a little bottle full of pills. It wasn't long before I was once again visiting other doctors, and I was soon right back where I had started. Then, I forged a prescription.

Chapter 18
All the Madmen

I would never make a forger. How I ever thought I could pass that prescription, I will never know. It was originally made out for steroids, but I erased that with an ink rubber and wrote '100 Dihydrocodeine' instead. You could clearly see where the words had been rubbed out; at one point, I had nearly gone through the paper, and of course there were none of the Latin abbreviations commonly used by doctors. I took the script to Boots because they were always busy, and I figured their pharmacist might not be so vigilant. You can imagine my surprise and delight when the prescription was dispensed. I still had to attend my normal weekly GP appointment to collect my real Dihydrocodeine prescription, and as soon as I walked in, I knew the game was up. My usual friendly doctor sat tight-lipped and grim. In front of him on his desk, looking even more amateurish than when I last saw it, was the forged prescription. My stomach dropped to my boots. In the end, the doctor was kind. He explained that he had no alternative but to report the matter to the police as it was a very serious matter. From that moment, I was put on to slow release Dihydrocodeine tablets. These would work in a similar way to methadone, delivering a steady dose of the drug without the 'high'. I was to start on eight 120mg tablets daily, and over time, this would be reduced. I was only given a day's worth of tablets at a time, and the prescription would be delivered directly to the pharmacy in Bishop's Waltham by the doctor. It has to be said that throughout my addiction to prescription drugs, my GP was absolutely fantastic. I like to think it was down to me that he boned up on drug addiction and became the surgery's resident expert. Just down the road there was a big drug rehabilitation centre called Alpha House. He saw a huge number of drug users from there. I had to see him each week on a Tuesday, and the waiting room was always full of thin, jumpy young men with dreadlocks and multiple piercings. I used to quite look forward to Tuesdays.

A few weeks later, a police car drew up outside our house. They had come to take me away. The officer was young, and from the way he drove, thought he was Nigel Mansell. At the police station they explained that if I were to be charged, it would be for the offence of 'uttering'. Can you believe that? It actually means the passing of a forged document. All the officers were very nice. I don't think I was their usual criminal type. I had a lengthy interview, and I think it was pretty obvious that I was just a very sad person who had done a stupid thing to acquire drugs purely for my own use. On the way back, the police radio suddenly burst into life. The driver announced that he was sorry, but we would have to divert to a house fire. On went the blues and twos, and off we shot. The fire had started in the kitchen of a thatched cottage in Wickham. We arrived at almost the same time as the fire engines. There was a considerable amount of black smoke, but I couldn't see any flames. I sat quietly in the back of the police car for about half an hour watching the unfolding drama. Eventually however, I was taken home. A couple of weeks later, I was summoned to the small police sub-station in Bishop's Waltham. The officer I saw was an older man, and he was very stern. They weren't going to be charging me. I was given a thorough ticking off, and he did say that if he ever saw me again, things would be very different. And with that, I was released back into the community. My brush with the law was the end of my various ruses to obtain Dihydrocodeine by deception. I settled into the regime of the slow release tablets. Before long, I was allowed to have a week's supply at once, and I was down to six 120mg tablets a day. It was a dose I would be stuck on for the next twenty years.

Tom and I soldiered on. Sadly, Godfrey died. He had gone into hospital for an exploratory operation as he was having difficulty swallowing. It was soon apparent he was riddled with cancer, and he was sent home to die. He only lasted two weeks before be passed. Tom hadn't been close to his father and didn't shed a tear. Come to think of it, I don't think Jane did either. She developed a definite spring in her step. After a break, I had gone back to work for Mike. Goodness knows why they took me back, but happily they did. At home, our family grew. We added a lilac point Siamese kitten to the gang. With her pointed face and big ears, she looked like a little white mouse. We called her Minnie. Tom absolutely doted on her and always called her 'Moo'. She gave us such a lift; for a while, we were almost happy again. That is until I started to drink.

My supply of painkillers now cut off, I quickly substituted one addiction for another. Like most addictions, it started gradually and ended up nearly killing me. I just didn't want to face the reality that was my life. Apart from our love of animals, Tom and I were such different people. Why had I ever thought we were such a good match? Cooking was the only thing we did together. Since Tom had Sky TV installed, and in particular Sky Sports, we even watched different TV's. I would perch on the stool in the kitchen and watch the portable, or go upstairs and watch the TV there. Tom would be in the front room all night glued to sport. He particularly liked golf and cricket. To me, watching cricket is like watching paint dry. And as for golf. Who in their right mind thought that would be a good sport to televise? You can't possibly follow the trajectory of the ball, and that polite ripple of applauds every time someone takes a shot sends me clean up the wall. When we first met, we had watched documentaries and hooted together at *Only Fools and Horses* and *Blackadder*. Those days were gone. We didn't like the same music. Tom actually liked Chris de Burgh. Oh, please. In my book, that's very nearly as bad as being a fan of Cliff Richard. I was into Radiohead, Oasis and Nirvana. So while I played *Smells Like Teen Spirit* and *Paranoid Android* on full volume, Tom was in another room humming along to *Lady in Red*. I didn't like his friends or their stuck up wives. Tom and I rarely saw our old group of friends now. We still only had the one car, and often when we did go out, we drove in a silent, horribly-heavy atmosphere. At least to me, it was horribly heavy. Tom more than likely didn't notice. Now she was on her own; we often went to Jane's for dinner. On one occasion, we were sat up at the table, and my depression and unhappiness suddenly overwhelmed me. I started to cry, and I had to get up from the table. Tom and his mother took absolutely no notice. They didn't ask me what was wrong, they made no comment at all, just carried on eating. I felt so alone. We were both incredibly disappointed with each other.

I felt that Tom wasn't a real man. He was frustrated that I wouldn't try to exercise and get myself healthy. I smoked like a chimney, I had abused my medication, and now it was dawning on him that I was drinking rather a lot of vodka. In hindsight, it was me who killed the marriage. Tom's love for me had once burnt so brightly. I alone doused the flames.

As soon as I got home from work, and Tom had gone to the pub, I would hit the vodka. I usually drank it with squash, but once Tom was home, I would have it with just plain tap water so it looked innocent. Every day I would buy a half bottle, and before long, the bottom of my wardrobe was full of empty bottles. I had loved the feeling I got from codeine, the detachment from reality, being somehow cushioned from life. Now vodka served the same purpose. At first, Tom didn't mention the fact that I was slurring my words and wobbling about, but it quickly started to cause rows. Most Fridays, I went to Vivienne's, and I looked forward to it immensely, as I could drink lots without being moaned at. I no longer partook of cannabis, but I more than made up for it in vodka. Soon I was in debt. I was spending at least £10.00 a day on booze and cigarettes. At the weekend, I was buying even more. I started to bounce cheques all around town. The shop owners would ring Tom, and he would have to go down and settle up with them. Bishop's Waltham is a small village, and we were both well known. It must have been dreadfully embarrassing for him. Several times he had to bail me out with the bank, which he could ill afford. He did try to talk to me. He tried to encourage me, but I was mired in alcohol and depression. At night, I would drink myself almost to oblivion. I was forever passing out with lighted cigarettes. Our three-piece suit was covered in burns. All the cushions had been turned at least once. All our bed covers were burnt; my pillow had large burn holes and so did the mattress. If it had been Tom falling around drunk and burning things, I would have gone mad. I'm not saying he was jumping for joy, but he put up with it. Tom had quite a well-stocked drinks cupboard, but I drank everything. He had several bottles of good whiskey which I drank and refilled with cold tea. The top was a bit frothy, but you would never have known at a glance it wasn't whiskey. Because he knew all my hiding places indoors, I had bottles hidden outside in all the bushes. I thought it ingenious, but speaking later with people who had been alcoholic, they pretty much all did the same thing. I started to drink at work, pouring the vodka into my tea and coffee. People always say vodka doesn't smell, but it's simply not true, you can smell the alcohol. No one said anything, probably because I kept my head down and didn't talk to anyone. But as soon as I got into the car at the end of the day, Tom would snarl, "You're drunk." Like alcoholics the world over, I spent my whole time splashing around in that well known Egyptian river. We usually rowed the whole way home. I wasn't eating. I got all my calories from drink. I started to look pallid and puffy. The mornings were terrible. As soon as I put the toothbrush into my mouth, I would start to retch. It was the worst thing. My eyes would be streaming, and I would dry heave until eventually I would bring up masses of bile, bright yellow and bitter. The only thing that settled my stomach was another drink. Weirdly, I took to watching Cartoon Network all the time. If I was home, I watched cartoons round the clock, and it would often be the same ones repeated over and over. I never watched anything else. I loved them. They comforted me. It was like I had reverted to being a child.

To make matters worse, my mother suddenly announced she was getting married again. She had mentioned a while back that she thought a funny little man was giving her the eye. They had gone out for one drink, he had proposed, and she had accepted. My aunt said he was a very nice man, but as usual, he had no property of his own and would be moving in with my mother. At first, I thought it was all a joke. I was mortified. My mother was seventy; she had been independent for years. This would be her fourth marriage. I just could not get my head round it. I couldn't imagine they could possibly be wanting to have sex. I didn't go to the wedding, and I didn't speak to my mother for a few years, until after her husband died in fact.

One morning we were driving into work when I suggested that as things were so bad we should get divorced. I often said this. It was my twisted way of getting reassurance from Tom. I used it as emotional blackmail. Tom always said no; he didn't want us to split. He loved me and we could work things out. This time he said, "I think it's probably a good idea." A few minutes passed, we had just pulled into the office car park when I said, "You're not seeing anyone else are you?" I honestly don't know what made me say it. I certainly had no suspicions. But Tom's silence said it all.

Chapter 19
Don't Speak

How I got through the day at work, I'll never know. Tom had the office next to mine, but his door remained firmly shut all day. Soon it was time to go home, and as you can imagine, the journey was pretty awful. To say I was devastated doesn't even come close. I was absolutely floored. I felt so betrayed. I had been so wrapped up in my own little world of misery, I hadn't given a thought to what Tom might be up to. She was a barmaid at the pub he went to each night. Her name was Kirsty. I called her Krusty. The affair had been going on for a couple of months. She had two young children, who Tom had grown to like. He had been to a school concert to see them perform. That really hurt. The pain was unbearable. Now, I suddenly remembered all the times he had quickly ended phone calls. All the times he had wandered outside with his phone. The constant ping of text messages that he said were from the lads. It all made sense. At first, Tom tried to tell me they hadn't slept together, but we both knew that wasn't true. For years, I had accepted that he didn't want to have sex, and now he was screwing someone else. All I could think of was them in bed together. It played over and over in my head. I didn't think I would ever recover. I remember screaming at him, "How could you do this to me." He looked at me so coldly. There was real hatred in his eyes; it was like a physical blow, and he said, "Well you did it." And he was right. Karma. What goes around comes around. I had hurt Danny like I was hurting now. I hadn't tried to work on our marriage. I had seen something better for myself, and I was off without a backward glance. However, that bit of insight didn't stop me from going on and on at Tom. What was she like in bed? Was she better than me? Did he enjoy it more? What positions had they done it in? Was she better looking? Was her body better? I was like a mad woman. When I asked him about the first time they had slept together, he did say rather stiffly, "It was all a bit of a failure if you must know." I didn't feel any better; they had obviously kept trying. As soon as we got home from work, he went off to the pub, and I hit the vodka. I decided I was going to turn up at the pub. Fuelled by the drink, I staggered down the road. I'm really not sure how I thought this was going to improve things, but through a fog of drink, a very bad idea can seem like a very good one. Tom and his friends were sitting at a table just by the pub entrance, and Tom's best mate Jamie spotted me immediately. He had the presence of mind to leap up and quickly usher me back out. Once outside, I broke down completely. Jamie hugged me and then surprised me by saying, "Don't worry, it's a fling. People have them. She's awful. She's a nutter. Tom will see her for what she is. Honestly, Ellie, it won't last." I have to say that cheered me up. What didn't cheer me up was finding out that Tom had done her conveyancing when she moved and that she had been into the office on more than one occasion. I was absolutely livid. The thought of them laughing and chatting in the office next to mine was almost more than I could take. And I bet he didn't charge her. I was so grateful to have Vivienne as a friend. She was a tower of strength and could find the funny side in almost anything. We often ended up joking about the whole sorry affair. I don't know what I would have done without her.

Jamie's prediction was spot on. After maybe a month I noticed Tom was no longer rushing to his phone whenever it bleeped, and he didn't answer when it rang. When our landline started to ring off the hook, he would say, "Leave it." Often it would ring throughout the night. If Tom wasn't in, I would sometimes pick up, and it would be her children. She actually got them to ring to ask when Tom was coming back. Then she started turning up at the house. I hadn't seen her before. She was as different to me as a person could be, and I wasn't altogether sure if that was good. She had dark hair and was not fat, but well built. I thought she was rather tarty. She wore a leopard print blouse, a black skirt and high heels. I noticed she was wearing an ankle chain. Tom went outside to speak to her. I didn't want him to. I wanted her to suffer, but I think he thought he owed her that. When he came back in, he looked at me a little sheepishly and said, "I think I've had a narrow escape." I almost felt sorry for him. Only Tom could have chosen a woman to have an affair with who was even crazier than me. After that, she showed up a couple more times and then she was gone. She handed in her notice at the pub. For a while, Tom and I united. For different reasons, we both realised it had been a narrow escape. I promised to sort out my drinking, he promised never to have another affair, and we both promised to work on our sex life. But it wasn't to be.

I finally did get help with my drinking. Once again my GP was marvellous. I did a home detox. I was prescribed a mild tranquiliser and a course of Vitamin B, and it was all relatively painless. Also, miracle of miracles, I had stopped smoking. I'm still not sure quite how I did it, I was practically a chain smoker, getting through thirty to forty menthol Superkings each day. We had been told our office was to become non-smoking within the next couple of months. I smoked all the time at work. I had an ashtray next to my computer. I knew I would either be permanently outside having fag breaks and wouldn't get any work done, or I would have to quit. I'm very much an all or nothing person. I can never understand people who can just have one or two chocolates from a box. If I have one, I have to eat the whole tray and more often than not, both trays. Sometimes, if Tom bought a cake or some nice biscuits, weeks later, I would see him rooting round in the cupboard looking for them. I had to tell him they didn't even make it to the cupboard. On my first day as a non-smoker, I stayed in bed for the entire day. I couldn't face doing anything or talking to anyone. I used nicotine patches and Nicorette chewing gum which really helped. When I woke in the morning, I was so buoyed at having gone a whole 24 hours without a cigarette, something I never dreamt possible; it spurred me on. And I haven't had a cigarette since. I was becoming a positive health freak. Tom had recently taken up cycling. He went for miles, right out into the country. He bought me a bicycle too. I think he was being a tad optimistic. It had thirteen gears which was twelve too many as far as I was concerned. I'd have liked an old school bike with a wicker basket and no gears. The new bicycle remained in the garage where (thank the Lord) the rabbits soon ate the tyres. As I was no longer drinking, Tom had bought himself a car, and I took over our old Citroen diesel. Life would be a lot easier now, we each had a car again.

1999 was drawing to a close, and a new century dawned. We had a couple of reasons to break out the champagne. My brother and his wife Kim were expecting their first child. They drove up to tell us the happy news. I was going to be an aunty and Tom an uncle. The other good news involved my sister Sarah. She had completed a chemistry degree as a mature student at Surrey University and got a first. It was an incredible achievement, and I was very proud of her. That New Year's Eve, we went to Tom's Golf and Country Club. It was an enormous bash. We had a brilliant time. As we watched the fireworks herald in the year 2000, I almost felt at peace with the world.

In early January, I got a call from Tom's gym. They said he had passed out in the shower and as a precaution, had been taken to hospital. When I arrived at the hospital, I got the distinct impression Tom wasn't at all pleased to see me. He wouldn't meet my eye, and he was grumpy and uncommunicative. He said it was all a fuss about nothing. He had passed out in the shower because he had exercised too hard and hadn't drunk any water. The guy at the gym agreed that was probably the reason. As soon as we got home, Tom went into the garden to talk on the phone. This had happened a couple of times lately. A few days back, I had seen him in the garden on his mobile. I had raced outside and asked him point blank, "Are you having another affair?" He got very cross and defensive and absolutely denied it. But I was suspicious. A horrible feeling of Deja vu washed over me and with it the realisation that once again Tom was seeing someone else.

Her name was Caroline. Different barmaid, same pub. And this time, I wasn't going to be rid of her so easily. She was popular, and Tom's friends all liked her. Tom said he loved her. He said he loved me as well. He said he was confused. Once again, my life was unravelling, and I geared myself up for a fight. Although I was furious with Tom, all my animosity was directed at her. Yet again, it was all about me not losing. It wasn't because I loved Tom. It was because I loved my way of life, and I wasn't going to let her beat me. It became, oh, so personal. At thirty-three she was younger than me, and I have to say, that stung. I got so fed up with Tom talking to her and texting her that I threw his mobile phone in the pond. Of course, he just got a new one.

Mainly because of the constant tirade of never-ending accusation from me, Tom moved to the spare bedroom. He should have known that moving to another room wasn't going to deter me. It was at the end of January when he wandered into our bedroom one evening and hovered in the doorway. Then he said, "I've got a tumour in my brain, and it's inoperable," and with that he was gone. He didn't come home that night. I began to think I had either misheard or misunderstood him. It was too much to take in. At work, he had a steady flow of clients, and his door was shut all day so I had to wait until we got home to tackle him. He told me that following his collapse the hospital had scanned his head and seen the tumour. They said it was a metastasis, a secondary cancer which had spread from its original site. In Tom's case, this was the mole which had been removed five years ago. Tom was very upbeat. He told me that although the doctors couldn't operate, they were going to get rid of the tumour with radiotherapy.

He continued to see Caroline. I tried everything I could think of to get him to finish with her. I pleaded and I threatened, but it had no effect. He wouldn't give her up. I knew Caroline was trying everything to get him to leave me. He stayed with me for a little while longer, but her pull was stronger. On Valentine's Day, I came home to find a note. He said he had gone to live with Caroline. He said it didn't mean it was over for us. He still loved me, but he needed some time to think. Good old Tom, walking out on Valentine's Day. And keeping his options open. I've got to say, I'd have preferred a bunch of flowers. Luckily, I've never liked Valentine's Day anyway. In my experience, you get all excited when you receive a card, only to find out later it's from the man down the road with no teeth and a comb-over.

Once again, I was nearly mad with grief and loss. I was sick with worry that Caroline would get pregnant. I was worried for the future, period. I couldn't believe this was happening again. I couldn't believe that Tom was dying although I knew full well he was.

Chapter 20
Didn't We Almost Have It All

Every weekend, I would pick Tom up from Caroline's flat, and we would do my main shop and get everything for the animals. Tom wasn't allowed to drive anymore in case he had a seizure. It had been a job getting him to surrender his car keys. In the end, Jamie had to act out the scenario of a child being killed before Tom would give them up. Shopping completed, Tom would come back with me, and we would clean out the rabbits and guinea pigs. I wouldn't have missed seeing him if only to get up Caroline's nose, but it was torture for both of us. I pleaded and pleaded for him to come home. If I wasn't pleading, I was railing against him. I feel thoroughly ashamed of myself now, but I was such a mess. I couldn't think straight and I wasn't rational. In Sainsburys, Tom would drive me nearly crazy because he kept putting things in the trolley for Caroline. She would give him a list containing things like tights, Lillets and *Hello* magazine. As fast as he put the items in the trolley, I would chuck them out. And I mean really chuck them. Being in the office together was also difficult. Tom still liked to get in early, so he got the bus each day. Before he moved in with Caroline, we used to nip in and out of each other's offices all the time and often ate our sandwiches together at lunchtime. Now his door was closed against me, and the whole office was subdued.

Tom started treatment. People tend to think of radiotherapy as the easy option. For Tom, it was pretty brutal. After each session, he got splitting headaches, and his scalp blistered. He was given a number one haircut, and it suited him. When I first met Tom, he had reminded me of Dustin Hoffman but with a moustache. As he aged, he came to more resemble a cross between Saddam Hussein and Hitler. His friends called him 'Boycie' because they thought him so like the character played by John Challis in *Only Fools and Horses*. Sometimes Caroline took him to hospital appointments, and sometimes I took him. She told them she was his partner. I told them I was his wife. It must have been very confusing for the consultant. He probably thought we were swingers. Tom was having frequent fits despite taking a drug to prevent them. Whenever he collapsed, he would also empty his bladder. We all told him it didn't matter, not one little bit, but you could see how distressing it was for him. It wasn't long before he had a seizure in the office. I heard a thump and raised voices. Several of us raced upstairs to find Tom on the floor in the small kitchen. He was only out for a couple of minutes, but he had wet himself, and it was pretty awful. I took him home. Well, back to Caroline's, which was where he insisted he wanted to be. Around this time, there was more sadness when our Burmese cat Oliver had to be put to sleep. I didn't tell Tom, he had enough on his plate. Vivienne held my hand. The vet came to the house, he knew me and Tom well. Bishop's Waltham being such a small place, he had heard about Tom's illness and probably his affair. He could see the state I was in. When I asked about the bill, he said, "There's no charge."

Every morning, when Caroline left for work, Tom would ring me. Usually he wanted a shoulder to cry on. Often he was upset about the constipation which had now begun to plague him, or he wanted advice about his frequent headaches. Whatever was bothering him, he would turn to me. He also moaned about Caroline's cooking. He was absolutely aghast that she didn't use garlic and went on about it at length. Tom and I put garlic in practically everything. Some of his Indian recipes called for entire bulbs. Naturally, I encouraged his disappointment in her lack of culinary expertise. I probably said, "I don't believe it," more times than Victor Meldrew. Other bones of contention were her poor sandwich making skills and that her flat had no Sky TV, no shower and no garden. And he missed 'Moo'. I immediately seized the opportunity to really piss her off and volunteered to make his sandwiches each day. From that day on, he lived with her, but I made his lunch. What eventually sealed Caroline's fate was when she invited Tom to Sunday dinner with her mother and father. I can only imagine what her parents made of their daughter dating a desperately sick married man, but apparently, they made him very welcome. The problem was they served roast beef, and they overcooked it. To Tom, this alone would have been sacrilege, but to add insult to injury, there was no horseradish, and the gravy was made with granules. This, Tom could neither excuse nor forgive. It was now Caroline's turn to be left a note, and he moved back in with me.

Following another seizure at work, the horrible decision was taken to tell Tom he could no longer practice as a solicitor. The firm would keep him on full pay indefinitely, and of course they all hoped he would visit. He must have been in utter turmoil, but he never once complained. I also had to stop working, as Tom couldn't be left on his own. I must say, the firm was absolutely wonderful. They kept me on full pay, which they were under no obligation to do, and I couldn't thank them enough.

Caroline was never going to go quietly. She bombarded Tom with calls. She seemed to have got it into her head that Tom had left to spare her the ordeal of looking after him. Knowing Tom as I did, that's almost certainly what he had written to her in his note. Maybe there was even some truth to it. She even got her father to ring Tom and beg him to reconsider. All Tom wanted was to be in his own home with the animals and garden he loved. Above all, he wanted some peace. Occasionally, he did take Caroline's calls. I would hear him say, "I can't. I can't," and deduced that she was either asking him to meet her, or to go back. To this day, I'm not sure what her motive was. She must have realised Tom was terminally ill and that time was running out. There was never going to be a happy ending. A few people thought she was after his money; it was all very strange. As Tom's illness progressed, I put my hatred of her to one side and suggested she could visit if Tom wanted to see her, but he said he didn't. After a while, she stopped calling, and I never heard him mention her again.

Tom never acknowledged that he was going to die. He talked all the time about the things he was going to do when he was better. He couldn't wait to drive again and to return to work. He talked about us renewing our vows and taking a long holiday in America. I don't think he believed it for a second. I think he was desperate for it to be true, to be happy again. He was an intelligent man. He must have known he wasn't going to recover. The doctors had informed him of the prognosis at the outset, but he chose to ignore it. When we went to the hospital, he refused to look at the scans of his brain. When the consultant held the images up to the light box, he would turn away. The fact that his illness was both virulent and untreatable was never mentioned. It made life extremely difficult. We didn't talk. We just pretended. We pretended that Tom was getting better, and we pretended we were in love. We had lived a lie for most of our marriage, and we couldn't seem to break the habit. It was tearing me apart. Sometimes I would look at Tom, and the pain in his eyes would make me flinch. I would have given anything to have the old Tom back. One warm night in July, we sat outside together on the patio, holding hands, quietly watching the bats. Suddenly he said, "You know this isn't the end," and he squeezed my hand. I said, "I know," and squeezed back. We were both too choked to say any more. At the end of July, it was Tom's forty-seventh birthday. We had a quiet meal out with friends. Tom had a fit in the restaurant. Whether it crossed his mind that this would be his last birthday, I don't know. But everybody else knew it.

Jamie helped us to dismantle our aquariums. We found homes for all the fish with aquatic shops in the area. We spent our days wandering around garden centres and craft shops. The irony is that we had probably never been so close. Tom's fits were increasing. I think he had a lie down just about in every garden centre in Hampshire and in most of the pubs. I got very twitchy when we were in amongst the ornaments or displays of china. Once people realised that Tom wasn't drunk, they were incredibly kind. Everybody was shocked and saddened to see such a relatively young man so ill. Tom was beginning to have spells of confusion and his speech was affected. He would suddenly talk nonsense and not seem to recognise people. His fits became more severe, and it was clear he was deteriorating. He still had a good appetite and enjoyed his food. He watched a lot of sport on TV, sitting contentedly with Minnie curled on his lap. He told me he thought she was a magic cat because whenever he picked her up, his headaches disappeared. He called her his 'Moo Guru'.

The hospital had now discharged him. There was nothing more they could do. We still saw the GP every couple of weeks. Tom was extremely unsteady on his feet, but he point blank refused to use a wheelchair. Jamie and I both tried to encourage him, but he was adamant he would never use one. His periods of lucidity were getting less. Macmillan nurses now came to watch him at night, so I could get some rest. The end of summer and the onset of autumn makes me melancholy at the best of times, but that year, it was dreadful. One day, Jamie came to take Tom out for a drive. At the front door, Tom wouldn't let go of me. He had me in a bear hug, like he was afraid to go. Jamie and I eventually coaxed him into the car. I watched as they drove away, and he looked so lost. They were only gone for about 30 minutes when Jamie brought him back. It was only when he got indoors that we realised he had gone out with his shoes on the wrong feet.

To give me a badly-needed break, the local hospice agreed to take Tom for a week. Jane and I dropped him off, and I left Jane with him whilst I came home. The next morning, Jane phoned to say she had been told that the hospice couldn't accommodate him after all. They had thought Tom would just lie in bed, dying quietly like all their other patients. Because Tom kept getting up and wandering, they simply didn't have the staff to watch him the whole time. When I arrived at the hospice, Tom clutched at me. He kept saying, "You left me. You left me." I felt terrible. Jane told me that when Tom was first admitted, just after I had left, he wet the bed. She said the nursing staff didn't make any attempt to hide their annoyance. One of them grabbed his arm and tried to pull him off the bed. I was furious, and I was near to breaking. What I called the hospice staff doesn't bear thinking about. I was hysterical. In between great wracking sobs I wailed, "This was supposed to be a fucking break for me, and you've fucking made things fucking worse. You're a load of fucking useless fucking bastards." I went on and on, long strands of snot dripping from my nose like slimy stalactites. To give them their due, the staff took it on the chin. I shouldn't have sworn at them, but surely they should have known how a person with a terminal brain tumour might behave. And where do people like Tom go when their carers need a break? I suppose they are heavily sedated so they can't cause inconvenience to anyone. Hospice policy required Tom to be transported in an ambulance, and we drove home in convoy, me leading the way through the country lanes. Tom was so happy to be home. As soon as he realised where he was, his whole face lit up. I felt happy too. It was where he was meant to be. Those were his last few lucid moments.

In October, Tom's brain ceased to function in any sort of cognitive way. To all intents and purposes, he was like someone with advanced dementia. He couldn't speak, and he didn't recognise anyone. He stopped eating, and the weight fell away. Where his hair had started to regrow, it was now completely grey, and he had a grey beard. He could no longer wash or brush his teeth. He did bizarre things. One time, he kept going into the kitchen and filling various receptacles with a mixture of cooking oil and water. There were bowls and jugs and cups all lined up, each filled to the brim. Another time, he drank a bottle of shampoo. You have never seen diarrhoea like it. The smell was truly horrendous. Jane was there, and the pair of us fell about, gagging and retching. Tom was caked in excrement. He had rubbed it everywhere. It was in his hair, over his face, under his nails. You name it, there was shit on it. Two young nurses arrived to help, and they were wonderful, so professional. They changed the bed and got him all cleaned up. I can't praise them highly enough. There was also the problem of Tom's frequent falls. Although by now, he was skeletal, he was still far too heavy for Jane or me to lift, even between us. The ambulance crew were marvellous. They would come out and pick him up. I could see in their eyes how sorry they were for all of us. Sometimes the ambulance would only just have gone when Tom would fall over again, so we had to call them back. If they minded, they never for a moment let it show. Tom also kept removing his clothes. He would constantly wander round, naked as the day he was born. I had to warn everybody who came to visit him lest they get a shock. I don't know why people with dementia always want to strip off, but for a person like Tom who had once been ultra-private and reserved, it was tragic. As Tom could no longer swallow medication, the nurses tried to fix a syringe driver to his back. It took them ages to set up, but no sooner had they finished, Tom would yank it out. They tried three times, then gave up.

Christmas rolled around, but there would be no celebrations. On Christmas morning, a friend from our Swanmore days arrived. I can't tell you how happy I was to see him, and I was touched he had taken time away from his family on Christmas Day. I was having a really difficult time with Tom. He kept getting out of bed and falling over. The ambulance had already been out twice. He fell again whilst John was there, but thankfully, John was able to haul him up and manoeuvre him onto the bed. I remember John's navy blue jumper being literally covered with Tom's dead skin. The ambulance men had earlier suggested calling Tom's GP for help. As John had to get back to his family and I couldn't deal with Tom on my own, we decided to do this. The doctor arrived quickly and gave Tom a large injection. The syringe was like something a horse vet would use. As the doctor was leaving, I said, "Is that it then? Will he get up again?"

The doctor squeezed my shoulder and said, "No, that's it now." That night, Tom's breathing became noisy. You could hear him all over the house. It was impossible to sleep. Early on Boxing Day evening, I had been on the phone to Sarah. As soon as we ended the call, I ran upstairs to check on Tom. Everywhere was silence, and I knew immediately that Tom was dead. I sat with him for just a few minutes. Not long at all. I didn't speak to him, I was numb with grief and shock. Then I rang Jamie who appeared almost immediately. He called the doctor and Tom's elder sister, so she could go round and break the news to Jane. He also called the undertaker. I didn't see them remove Tom's body. I was in the kitchen, and Jamie closed the door. I did however watch the small van as it pulled around the corner and carried Tom away from home for the very last time.

Chapter 21
Nevermore

Tom's funeral was a really big affair. The church was packed; people were standing in the aisles. So many people wanted to say goodbye. Keith gave the eulogy. It was extremely moving but often funny. At times, the church was filled with laughter. Keith's speech was so good; when he had finished, he was given a standing ovation. Even the vicar was clapping. He looked a bit pissed off. I bet he was thinking he had never seen the church so full and that his own sermons didn't go down anywhere near as well. Tom was being buried with only close friends and family attending. I couldn't bear the thought of a cremation. That dreadful moment when the curtains closed, I remembered my nan's funeral and how awful it was. Bishop's Waltham Cemetery is a beautiful spot. It's known to be frequented by deer, who make short work of any fresh flowers left on the graves. Tom would have loved that. On January 4, 2001, he was laid to rest. I remember reading about a 16th century Queen of Castile called Juana. She had married the son of the Holy Roman Emperor Maximilian I, called Philip the Handsome. I suspect his mother might have had something to do with the moniker, or it was given him by his courtiers. They would hardly have called him Philip the Dog Rough (not to his face anyway). Anyway, when he died, aged only twenty-eight, Juana became so unhinged that she insisted on the coffin being opened whereupon she threw herself onto the corpse. It was only with difficulty that she was parted from it. I knew exactly how she felt. I didn't feel inclined to demand the coffin be opened, but just for a moment, I thought it a real possibility I might pitch myself into the hole on top of it and have to be forcibly prised off. After the burial, we all went back to the restaurant in Bishop's Waltham where just a few months before we had celebrated Tom's birthday. They put on a wonderful spread, although, I couldn't face eating.

The next few days passed in a blur. I had been running on empty for so long, I was a complete wreck physically and mentally. During Tom's last months I had started drinking again. Not nearly so much as before. I had to stay relatively sober to look after Tom. When he died, there were lots of morphine tablets left, and I'm proud to say I handed them in at the pharmacy. There was a time when I would have been planning a party. I didn't want to go back to work. Tom was such a big presence in the office. I couldn't face seeing a new solicitor in his room, sitting at his desk. The firm were happy to let me go. I'm sure they were relieved. I was desperately unhappy. Tom's two affairs played in my head constantly. I couldn't blame him for his infidelity. It's easy to take the moral high ground when the opportunity to stray has never arisen. After years without intimacy, if a man had paid me a lot of attention and treated me like a princess, I would have taken a flyer. And knowing me, I would have fallen madly in love. So many people told me that it was because Tom had a brain tumour that he was unfaithful, but I knew it wasn't true. In my heart, I knew Tom hadn't wanted to be with me. It was all a sham. He had left Caroline because her flat was small, and he wanted to spend his last days in his own beautiful home. If he didn't have cancer, he would have ridden off into the sunset with her, of that I have no doubt. She would have had to have brushed up on her cookery and learnt to like garlic, but they would have been happy. I knew he had been incredibly fond of me and I knew he would have always looked out for me. I like to think we would have remained friends. These thoughts now crowded my head. I just had to learn to live with them.

Soon, all the well-wishers and visitors fell away, and I was left alone. During Tom's illness, I had patched things up with my mother. Her husband had also died of cancer, so there seemed little reason for us to be estranged. She and my aunt were such a help. They came up a couple of times a week to help me with the guinea pigs and our one remaining rabbit. They helped me with the housework and tried to lift my spirits. I was worried about Morph and Gizmo who had begun to mess around in the house. Whether it was because their routine had been upset or because so many strangers were constantly in the house, I don't know, but it was a big problem. I paid a lot of money for an expert in cat behaviour to come to the house. Talk about stating the bloody obvious. He didn't tell me anything about cats that I didn't already know. I put more dirt trays down, but still they messed about. They peed so often in the hall that the laminated floor began to warp. They peed on my duvet and on my clothes if I left them out. The house began to stink of cat pee. One day, I came home to find a large puddle on the gas hob. After a while, they started to poo as well as pee. I took them to the vet, but he couldn't find anything wrong. I knew it couldn't continue. Once again, the vet came to the house, and my two little Devon Rex brothers were put to sleep. I don't think I have ever felt so miserable. I could still cry about it now, but really, I didn't have a choice.

A friend of Tom's who owned his own estate agency came to see me one day, and he threw me a lifeline. He had not long lost his own father to cancer, so he knew how I was feeling. He offered me a job in Fareham working in the survey department, typing building surveys and Homebuyer Reports. I enjoyed the work, and I got on well with Alison, the other girl who worked there. We went to see Joe Jackson at Portsmouth Guildhall. It was my third time of seeing him, and as ever, he was excellent. But I was really struggling. I remained on a high dose of Dihydrocodeine, I was drinking too much, and I was deeply depressed. My hands were in a terrible state. Sometimes after typing several long reports, the pain was unbearable. I noticed that my fingers were beginning to lock and were splaying sideways at an odd angle. It was obvious that something was very wrong. One day, I had a terrible row with Alison. It was mostly my fault. I completely lost it and I ended up walking out. In my defence, I shouldn't have been working. I was in a sorry state, mentally and physically. It was all too much too soon. Days later, I woke one morning to find I could no longer straighten my fingers. In fact, apart from my index fingers, I couldn't move them at all. My typing days were over.

Tom's death should have left me comfortable. The house was now mortgage free, and it was worth a lot. Tom had several policies which had paid out on his death. If I had been able to carry on working, today I would be a lady of means. I had nobody to turn to for advice, and as the saying goes, "A fool and his money are easily parted." Sadly, I am that fool. I've got the t-shirt. I think it runs in the family. Over the years, with the exception of my brother, we've all worked our way steadily down the property ladder. Money certainly drips through my fingers. Because I had over the allowance, I wasn't eligible for benefit. It took me ages to be accepted for disability living allowance so I had nothing coming in. I had to live off my capital, which is never a good idea. The house was big and so were the bills. The rates alone were enormous. After a couple of years of trying to hold on, I knew I had to sell up. By now, the guinea pigs had all died, and there was only the one rabbit. A friend of a friend offered him a home where I knew he would be happy. Of the cats, Cleo had died some time ago and only Minnie and Star remained. The day I exchanged contracts, I honestly felt like jumping off a cliff. I had mixed feelings about leaving. I remembered standing in the back garden at night looking in at the house which was beautifully lit. Through the leaded diamond windows, I could see the bright décor within, the artwork and the sparkling chandeliers. I couldn't believe how lucky I was to be living in such a gorgeous house. There had been happy times, cooking with Tom, gardening together, stocking the pond and mucking out the animals. But there were an awful lot of bad times which were too painful to remember. It was time for a fresh start.

Chapter 22
Hide in Your Shell

I moved with Minnie and Star to a large detached property in Lee-on-the-Solent, where I had once been so happy. I loved Bishop's Waltham, but it was terribly expensive, and I was a long way from my family. My aunt and uncle lived in Lee, and mother, James and Annie were in nearby Gosport. Sarah was in the same cottage in Haslemere but not for much longer. She and David had parted ways. Not long after they split, she took up with a rather wealthy banker who she had met when they were both walking their dogs. Once again, he was very quiet, but he was intelligent and certainly more mature than David. For a time, it would seem they were well matched.

My new house was in a shabby condition. An elderly couple had lived there for many years, and it needed modernising. However, I could easily have lived in it as it was, and if I had any sense, that's what I should have done. But in my normal fashion, I wanted everything beautiful and perfect instantly. That meant a new kitchen and bathroom, new carpets throughout and the whole house redecorated with no expense spared. My uncle knocked down the ancient greenhouse and constructed a lovely 'L'-shaped pond where it had once stood. I now had a very desirable property but no money. All the money I had spent had been on cosmetic improvements, I should have seen to the bigger more important repairs. For instance, the brickwork was in a terrible state and badly needed to be repointed. The drains needed repair, and several of the windows needed replacing.

I registered with the GP in Lee-on-the-Solent. I was still taking six 120 mg slow release Dihydrocodeine tablets a day, and he insisted that we very gradually start to reduce the dose. I was taking a daily antidepressant and for the lupus, an immune-suppressive medication called Azathioprine. My hands were completely crippled. The orthopaedic surgeon at the hospital thought it may be possible to straighten my fingers, at least slightly. She also wanted to replace my knuckles, as I was getting so much pain. When it came to straightening my fingers, the operation wasn't a success; they immediately reverted to the same curled position. However, the replacement knuckles have worked a treat, and my hands no longer cause me any pain. Whilst under the anaesthetic, my left hand little finger was amputated, as it was lying at such an odd angle. I also had some metalwork put in both thumbs. I do have the use of my index fingers and thumbs on both hands, so I can still one-finger type. Just don't ask me to high five or clap.

Vivienne had met the man she was to marry. I saw less of her now. She had been such a good friend. If I'm honest, I think when I stopped drinking so much and gave up cannabis, all of a sudden, we had less in common. We had enjoyed getting wrecked together, being sober wasn't nearly such fun. The phone calls between us became fewer and fewer, especially once she had fallen madly in love with her man. I have to say, I was bitterly disappointed that I wasn't invited to their wedding. They went off to Scotland, and I know it was a very quiet affair, but I would have loved to have wished her well. I'm sorry we lost touch, and I hope she has been happy. For my part, once again I was mired in depression. It felt like I was being followed by my own personal black cloud. The GP arranged for me to see a psychiatrist, but I didn't find it helpful. These people only seem to be happy when they have made you break down. I didn't want to be made to cry. I knew that if I started, I would never stop. There were things in my head I didn't want to face. I've always been the same. I prefer to bury things; the deeper, the better. It's not healthy, I know, but it's a hard habit to break. Once, in the wee small hours, I did ring the Samaritans. Now I'm not saying they don't do an excellent job, but they are totally fixated on whether you are contemplating suicide. You can almost feel their disappointment when you answer 'No' when asked if you are suicidal. You can imagine the slump of the operator's shoulders. I got the distinct impression that if I had answered 'Yes', he would have mouthed, "I've got one," to his colleagues and punched the air, maybe done a little jig.

I thought a lot about death and the finality of it all. Funerals are funny things. I'm sure I'm not the only one who whenever they hear the words 'Ashes to ashes' mentally sings *Funk to funky*. At Tom's funeral, several of his friends threw golf balls in on top of the coffin. Did they really think he would be playing a round of golf in heaven? What did they think he was going to use for a club? I'm not really a believer in heaven or hell. If they do exist, then hell sounds much more like where the party is. And it would definitely be warmer. I like to think that somewhere in an alternate universe, Elvis and Bowie are rocking out together. John Lennon on rhythm guitar, George Harrison on lead, Beethoven playing piano. Maybe Freddie Mercury and Tom Petty on backing vocals with Mozart conducting. It's a nice thought, but I think it's much more likely we just become fertilizer. After Tom died, a friend of mine suggested we go see a medium. I don't think so. Tom didn't speak to me when he was alive. I hardly think he was going to suddenly become chatty once he was dead. He'd probably say, "I'll call you back." Mediums never tell you anything thing useful. They should be asking the dearly-departed questions like, "Where are you? What it's like? Who are you with? Have you met Jesus?" Instead they say, "I've got Percy here for Pamela. He's telling me you once had a watch with a blue strap." It's really all bollocks. When the cemetery groundsmen excavated Tom's grave, they made enough room for my coffin when the time comes. All I can say is, Tom's going to get a very unpleasant surprise when I land on top of him. My funeral song is going to be the Jam's *Going Underground.* I've no objection if the church organist wants to have a crack at it, so long as he plays loud. I get very annoyed when church hierarchy refuse to allow the bones of long dead historical figures to be examined, especially when they are several hundred years old. If they truly believe our spirit ascends to heaven, then surely our skeleton is surplus to requirements. The skulls should be used for forensic facial reconstruction, like they did with Richard III. Anne Boleyn would be a perfect candidate. The few extant portraits of her are wooden and not at all lifelike. It's hard to imagine what the flesh and blood woman would actually have looked like. Dig her up I say, let the forensic artists have a go. If she was looking down from heaven, I bet she would be chuffed to bits. I think the skulls of all historical figures should be used for facial reconstruction, unless really good portraits of them exist of course. Nobody raises any objection to Tutankhamun being subjected to scans, prodded about and put on display. His remains have been so manhandled over the years, bits of him have dropped off. May I state for the record that should anyone ever want to dig up my old skull in the interests of science or just to use the eye sockets as tea light holders, it's not a problem, fill your boots.

My lupus was active again. So much so that my GP arranged for carers to come in twice a day to help me with dressing, undressing and washing. I know it's a pretty thankless job, but in my opinion, some of the carers could have done with carers. I would struggle to say they were better than nothing. The whole operation was badly run. One carer told me that travelling wasn't taken into account when the daily rota was prepared. So after the first call, they were already running late. All their subsequent patients were understandably either cross, distressed or both. More often than not, the carer who was supposed to help me get up in the morning didn't arrive until gone midday. It was hopeless. I had a key safe installed by the front door, which I had to pay for myself. The idea is that the carers punch in a code, get the key and let themselves in. Despite telling them all a million times, the carers still ignored the key safe and rang the bell. It made me really cross. Then one of them used the key from the key safe and promptly lost it. That was the end for me. I had the lock changed and told the agency I wouldn't be needing them anymore. I spent most of my days in bed, only getting up to go to the loo or feed the cats. I had nothing else to get up for. I slept for most of the day and then watched TV or read into the early hours. Often I didn't speak to anyone for days. I couldn't manage the housework, and I had to pay a chap to keep the garden from becoming a jungle. The big lawn always seemed to need cutting and the tall privet hedges which surrounded the property required almost constant trimming.

Minnie and Star lived on for three years, but then within six months of each other, they were gone. They were my last link to Tom, and their deaths were particularly tough. But they had both lived long and happy lives so I had to be content with that. A friend took me to buy a little grey tabby Devon Rex kitten who I named Pasha. Shortly afterwards, Pasha was joined by a lilac point Siamese called Lily. After five years in the property, I had to face the fact that I would have to downsize. I simply couldn't afford to stay on. If only I had moved into a smaller property in the first place, I would have saved myself a ton of money and the heartache of leaving yet another home. I soon found a small terraced house, still in Lee-on-the-Solent, but no longer in the posh part. It was over a hundred years old and had once been a fisherman's cottage, so it was quaint. It was in terrible condition, having been a rental property for many years. The firm my brother works for carried out the renovations. The whole house was gutted. I boarded the cats for the first three weeks, whilst the worst of the work was carried out. The whole project took a couple of months to complete. I thoroughly enjoyed having the builders around. They made me laugh with their constant banter. I felt quite bereft when they had gone. I had to get rid of a lot of my possessions, I simply didn't have the space for all the ornaments and furniture. My cousin's wife and I did a few car boot sales. Mandy had to keep a tight rein on me, otherwise her van would have been more loaded going than coming. I bitterly regret that I took all my albums to a charity shop. Especially now everybody wants albums. I know I could rebuy my favourites, but it wouldn't be the same. I had owned some of the Bowie albums since I was twelve. They had been played thousands of time and seen me through so much. After Tom died, I simply couldn't listen to music. Any music. I lost ten years. Music made me far too emotional. I didn't think I would ever enjoy music again, and it was that which prompted me to give away all my LPs.

Settled into my new home, I soon reverted to staying up all night and sleeping all day. I was eating all the wrong things. I would take food up to eat in bed, whole packets of biscuits and large slabs of white chocolate. I would fry slices of bread in butter and drizzle on golden syrup. I began to pile on weight, putting on three stones. In a short time, I went from a size 8-10 to a 14-16. I lived in leggings and shapeless tops. I was fat and fifty. Actually, I was fat and fifty-five which is even worse. I was completely reclusive, only leaving the house if it was absolutely necessary. I didn't wash, and I didn't clean my teeth. Sometimes I would go several weeks without having a bath. I could smell myself, and my skin was dry and cracked. Because I lay in bed all day, I lost the little bit of muscle I had. I was so weak. If I had to stand in a queue at the supermarket, I would have to lean on something to support myself. I drove everywhere, even really short distances because I was too weak to walk. I had chronic constipation and chronic lower back pain. I felt like my life was over. I was waiting to die.

Chapter 23
Here Comes the Sun

The one person who I did talk to was Sarah. Every couple of weeks, she would ring and try to encourage me out of my lassitude. Sarah has a great joy for living, always looking to the future. My inclination is to yearn for the past, and I know it exasperates her beyond belief. Being a scientist, she's very knowledgeable about health and issues pertaining to it. I think she probably reads *The Lancet* or *The Prick It*, whatever the medical journal is called. Most people are now aware that it is sugar causing the obesity epidemic, not fat. Everyone has jumped on the bandwagon, but Sarah gave me the heads up seven years ago. Amazingly, some GP's are still banging on about low fat diets and how fat is the enemy. One day, with Sarah's displeasure at my lifestyle choices still fresh in my mind, I thought I would try walking to the local shops. The shops are a very short distance away, about five minutes is all. My concern was that although I might be able to get there, I wouldn't have the energy to get back. That's how feeble I was. But I made it, and it gave me a real lift. I was proud of myself. Now I took the decision to give up sugar. And after only a few days, I found I wasn't missing it in the least. I became a bit fanatical, scanning food labels to look for sugar. It's in pretty much everything, even pork pies can you believe. The only thing I still allow myself are baked beans, but only occasionally. The weight fell off. It was like magic.

The next time I walked to the shops, I bumped into a young man who was putting leaflets through doors offering people help with technology. I had a chat with him about my rather pitiful IT skills, and he gave me his card. I had bought a laptop when I moved, but I wasn't using it. I decided to give him a call to get some help. He was brilliant. Kevin, I can never thank you enough. He also loved music, and that very day, at his suggestion, I ordered myself an iPod. Meanwhile, he showed me how to download the few CDs I had onto my computer and how to burn new ones so I could make compilations for the car. Gradually I repurchased all my old favourites. Suddenly, music was back in my life. When my iPod arrived, I downloaded music like a thing possessed. I caught up with some of the groups I had missed, the Arctic Monkeys, Foo Fighters, Elbow, Train, M83, AltJ the wonderful Muse; the list is endless. I made hundreds of playlists and bought some Bluetooth headphones so I could listen to them while walking. My taste in music is eclectic, anything from Sinatra to Soundgarden. I live in fear that I'll collapse out walking one day and someone will pick up my iPod to find it playing *Je t'aime* or *On the Trail of the Lonesome Pine*. I try to walk for at least an hour a day, and I am so much stronger. I go regularly to the gym, and I swim with friends every Monday. My twenty-five-year dependency on prescription painkillers is also a distant memory. I haven't taken a Dihydrocodeine pill for nearly six years now. I still have a large supply, but I've never been in the least bit tempted. I like to have them in reserve, in case I get any signs of dementia. Then I'm going to take the whole lot—quickly. Although my health has improved beyond belief, it hasn't all been plain sailing. Continuous use of steroids over the years has left me with osteoporosis. I've had to have operations on both of my feet. I also had my gallbladder removed because of gallstones. The GP sent me to have an ultrasound just to confirm the diagnosis. I sat with several young women who were pregnant and positively glowing. They sat smiling serenely nursing their bumps, and I sat grimacing nursing my gallstones. I bet I know who's got the better pelvic floor though.

Once my manky gallbladder had been taken out, my health continued to improve. So much so that I began to feel uncomfortable being on benefits. Also, I was bored with doing nothing all day. I saw a notice in the Job Centre about a charity that gets people who have been on long term disability benefits back into work. Tania, the lady who works for the charity, was wonderful. She is the type of person you would want to have as a best friend. After a couple of months, she got me an interview with a government organisation for a six-month placement. The charity would pay my wages during that time and then hopefully, the organisation would keep me on. Tania came with me for the interview. I was bricking it. I hadn't worked for the best part of seventeen years. Computers had only just come in when I was last in a working environment. I booked myself some driving lessons, to give me the confidence to negotiate the three large roundabouts on the journey in, should I be offered a job. I'm delighted to say they did take me on, and I have since passed a further interview and been employed permanently. I only do two days a week, which is enough. I couldn't manage full time. I love being at work again. The team I work with have made me so welcome, I am eternally grateful. I do have to keep reminding myself that I'm there to work and not just to socialise, but they put up with me. And I never did manage those roundabouts. I take the scenic route.

I see a lot of my aunt. She is ninety and as fit as a fiddle. We often go to the theatre or take a coach trip somewhere. My uncle is also well into his eighties but still works as a builder. He's the first port of call when anything goes wrong in the house. He recently came and unblocked my drains, poor devil. Nowadays, neither of them drink more than the odd glass of wine. Although, it hasn't escaped my notice that at the theatre, come the intermission, my aunt is out of her seat like a greyhound from a trap to get to the bar first.

I see a good deal of my brother and his family. Kim often takes mother and me to visit National Trust properties in the area. Her two boys come too. Well, Alex always comes. Sebastian has to be surgically removed from his Xbox, but occasionally, he joins us. Typical teenage boys, they have me in stitches because I, of course, am sixty going on twelve. I don't have to stoop to their level, I'm on it. I do despair over Alex's musical taste. I had a little more hope for Sebastian. When he was ten, for a while he liked Bon Jovi and Bruce Springsteen, but I expect that's now fallen by the wayside.

Every week I take mother shopping. She's eighty-eight and still bright and active. She has had a bad hip but refuses to see a doctor. It can take us quite a while to get round the supermarket. I like to keep her moving, lest she catches the eye of some elderly gentleman and gets any ideas. She is still burning toast.

After years of being on her own, my sister Annie has met a nice man, and they are planning to buy a house together.

I didn't keep in contact with Tom's mother. Shortly after he died, I found out that he had taken Caroline to Jane's for Sunday dinner. It was when their affair had just started, and he was still living with me. I couldn't forgive Jane; it was too much of a betrayal. Over the years, we had become friends. She took me to nearly all my chemotherapy appointments, and I thought we had bonded. I felt she should have told Tom she would be happy to meet his new girlfriend, but first he must end things with me. No doubt, Tom inherited his inability to say no from her.

I speak to Sarah often. We are very different people, but we find common ground and get along well most of the time. She is so clever. She will sometimes ring or text me to say, "Ellie, you must listen to Mozart's piano concerto No. 23 in A, K488," and I'm thinking *I just paused Backstreet Boys to answer this*. Sadly, her relationship with the banker didn't work out. Our bad luck seems to run in tandem. Her dog Molly recently died of liver failure. She was old, but naturally, Sarah was devastated. A week later, I lost my little Devon Rex Pasha. She had cancer and had to be put to sleep. She was eleven so I had hoped for another couple of years with her. She had sat next to my computer whilst I wrote most of this book, and at first, I didn't think I had the heart to carry on with it. Now I play Neil Young's *Long May You Run* for her and remember the joy she brought me. And of course, I still have my beautiful Lily.

Last year, I bumped into Aaron, and I've seen him a couple of times since. He has his own company and is doing well. He's lost his hair but still has a twinkle in his eye. It was as if years just rolled away. I could have still run off with him, although, I doubt we'd fit in a bath together nowadays. As we were talking, I wondered if he remembered all the things we got up to those forty years ago. I doubt it, men aren't sentimental. Anyway, we chatted politely and it was wonderful to see him. He's still goofing on Elvis which is nice.

Fate is a strange thing. I must have passed my little house hundreds of times when I was a kid. I had to cycle by it to call for Sylvia. I could never have known back then that it was where I would end up. It's a strange feeling. For the main, I'm very happy. I stride around Lee, headphones on, past places where I played so happily as a child. I still like my music loud, so I'll probably need a hearing aid any time soon. I walk alone, but sometimes I'm accompanied by ghosts. Ghosts of long-dead loves and animals and opportunities. Every now and again, I'm crushed by memories and feelings of loneliness, and I could curl into a ball and howl. So if anyone knows an ageing hippy who can play *Give a Little Bit* on the acoustic guitar, or *Yakety Sax* on the yakety sax, then get in touch. I'm a terrific cook, and I put out on the first date.

So, what have I learnt? That you should never sell yourself cheaply, get married at nineteen, or settle for a bad relationship because you think it's better than being alone. I've learnt that you can never listen to too much Radiohead, and, although it's a long time since I last saw one, I've learnt that penises aren't hairy.